Disney·PIXAR

Story Collection

5 Stories

1

길벗스쿨

Disney·Pixar Story Collection 1

초판 발행 • 2022년 11월 22일 | **발행인** • 이종원 | **발행처** • 길벗스쿨
주소 • 서울시 마포구 월드컵로 10길 56(서교동) | **대표 전화** • 02)332-0931 | **팩스** • 02) 323-0586
홈페이지 • www.gilbutschool.co.kr | **이메일** • gilbutschool@gilbut.co.kr
기획 및 책임편집 • 이경희(natura@gilbut.co.kr), 한슬기, 임채원 | **디자인** • 이현숙 | **제작** • 이준호, 손일순, 이진혁
영업마케팅 • 김진성, 박선경 | **웹마케팅** • 박달님, 권은나 | **영업관리** • 정경화 | **독자지원** • 윤정아, 최희창
한글 번역 • 최주연 | **영문 감수** • Ryan P. Lagace | **전산편집** • 연디자인 | **녹음** • YR미디어 | **CTP 출력 및 인쇄** • 교보피앤비 | **제본** • 경문제책

▶ 잘못 만든 책은 구입한 서점에서 바꿔 드립니다.
▶ 이 책은 저작권법에 따라 보호받는 저작물이므로 무단전재와 무단복제를 금합니다.
　이 책의 전부 또는 일부를 이용하려면 반드시 사전에 저작권자와 길벗스쿨의 서면 동의를 받아야 합니다.

ISBN 979-11-6406-448-9 64740 (길벗 도서번호 30515)
　　　979-11-6406-447-2 64740 (세트)

정가 22,000원

제 품 명	: Disney·Pixar Story Collection 1
제조사명	: 길벗스쿨
제조국명	: 대한민국
전화번호	: 02-332-0931
주　소	: 서울시 마포구 월드컵로 10길 56 (서교동)
제조년월	: 판권에 별도 표기
사용연령	: 8세 이상

KC마크는 이 제품이 공동안전기준에
적합하였음을 의미합니다.

CONTENTS

Disney · PIXAR
Story Collection 1

COMPONENTS

Main Book
5 popular stories based on Disney movies

인기 많은 디즈니 애니메이션 영화 5편의 내용을 한 권에 담은 콜렉션입니다. 영화 장면을 생동감 있게 표현한 일러스트와 오리지널 스토리를 가장 충실하게 녹여낸 문장으로, 원서 읽는 즐거움뿐만 아니라 영어 실력까지 향상시킬 수 있습니다.

Characters & Key Words

알아두면 원서 읽기가 쉬워지는 단어들을 선별했습니다. 등장인물들의 이름 표기와 맥락 이해에 중요한 역할을 하는 키워드 40개를 학습해 보세요.

캐릭터

키워드

MP3 Audio Files

QR코드를 스캔하면 아래의 음원을 들으면서 학습할 수 있습니다. 스트리밍 듣기 또는 전체 파일 다운로드가 가능합니다.

🔑 Key Words
📖 Story Reading

바로 듣기

길벗스쿨 e클래스
eclass.gilbut.co.kr → 학습 자료실

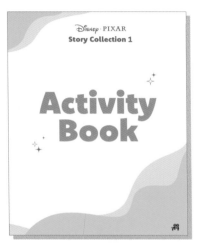

Activity Book
Includes book quizzes, questions for words, sentences, details and reading skills

스토리를 읽고 나서 얼마나 잘 이해했는지 진단하는 북 퀴즈를 제공합니다. 15개의 문제를 풀어 보고, 맞힌 개수를 확인해 보세요.
액티비티 파트에서는 다양한 유형의 연습문제를 접하며 단어, 문장구성, 세부적인 내용 이해뿐만 아니라 글의 전체 구조까지 파악하는 힘을 기를 수 있습니다.

| Word Check | Story Check | Sentence Check | Story Map |

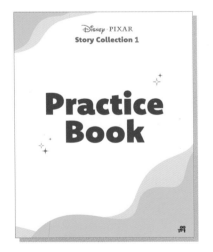

Practice Book
for word & sentence practice

어휘력과 문장력을 강화하는 연습용 워크북이 제공됩니다. 각 장면에 등장하는 어휘의 철자와 뜻을 정확히 익히는 단어 연습장과 빈칸을 채워 문장을 완성하는 문장 완성 연습장으로 이뤄집니다. 문장 완성 연습장은 본책 스토리의 우리말 뜻을 확인하는 해석본으로 사용할 수 있습니다.

| Word Practice | Sentence Practice |

HOW TO READ

❧ 영어 실력이 한 단계 업그레이드 되는 원서 읽기 ❧

Step 1. 워밍업, 키워드 살펴보기

책을 읽기 전, 내용 파악에 핵심적인 역할을 하는 단어들을 미리 살펴보세요. 스토리에 등장하는 주요 캐릭터들의 이름을 확인하고, 내용을 예측해 봅니다.

Step 2. 집중 듣기

손으로 단어를 짚어가면서 원어민 성우의 음성을 귀 기울여 들어 보세요. 이런 집중 듣기를 통해 낯선 단어가 어떻게 발음되는지 정확하게 알 수 있으며, 음원의 속도에 맞추어 눈으로 읽어 내려가는 연습을 하다 보면 많은 양의 글을 빠르고 정확하게 읽을 수 있는 능력이 길러집니다.

Step 3. 소리 내어 읽기

소리 내어 읽어 보세요. 소리 내어 읽을 때 눈으로 보는 텍스트와 귀로 듣는 소리가 연계가 되고, 반복하여 읽을수록 읽는 속도와 정확성이 향상됩니다. 이런 과정에서 단어와 문장 구조를 인지할 수 있고, 뜻을 기억해내며 독해력을 발달시킬 수 있습니다.

Step 4. 북퀴즈로 이해도 확인하기

스토리의 내용을 얼마나 파악했는지 북퀴즈를 풀어 점검해 보세요. 맞힌 개수가 적다면 스토리북을 꼼꼼히 다시 읽으면서 정확히 이해할 수 있도록 합니다.

Step 5. 워크북 학습하기

Activity Book을 풀이하며 스토리의 세부내용을 살펴보고, 스토리에 담긴 영어 표현과 문장 구조를 익히는 시간을 가져 보세요.
또한 Practice Book을 통해 어려웠던 단어나 의미를 분명히 알지 못했던 단어를 별도로 학습하며 어휘력을 높이고, 문장 하나 하나의 정확한 의미를 확인해 보세요.

Characters

Baymax

Hiro

Tadashi

Yokai

Callaghan

Abigail

Key Words

☐ create	통 만들어내다	☐ professor	명 교수
☐ invention	명 발명품	☐ impress	통 감명을 주다
☐ invent	통 발명하다	☐ accident	명 사고
☐ nurse	통 간호하다 명 간호사	☐ left	leave(떠나다)의 과거형
☐ name	통 이름을 짓다 명 이름	☐ discover	통 발견하다
☐ allow	통 가능하게 하다	☐ villain	명 악당
☐ tiny	형 아주 작은	☐ attack	통 공격하다
☐ machine	명 기계	☐ barely	부 간신히, 가까스로
☐ mircobot	명 초소형 로봇	☐ escape	통 탈출하다 명 탈출
☐ object	명 물건, 물체	☐ life	명 목숨, 생명

Key Words

- [ ] **plan** 	명 계획
- [ ] **high-tech** 	형 최첨단의
- [ ] **suit** 	명 (특정한 활동에 입는) 옷
- [ ] **fist** 	명 주먹
- [ ] **secret** 	형 비밀의
- [ ] **laboratory** 	명 실험실
- [ ] **portal** 	명 (다른 세계로 통하는) 관문
- [ ] **enter** 	동 들어가다
- [ ] **risky** 	형 위험한
- [ ] **mission** 	명 임무

- [ ] **revenge** 	명 복수
- [ ] **responsible** 	형 책임이 있는
- [ ] **bravely** 	부 용감하게
- [ ] **rescue** 	동 구출하다 명 구출
- [ ] **damage** 	동 피해를 입히다
- [ ] **last** 	명 마지막 남은 것
- [ ] **blast** 	동 발사하다
- [ ] **safe** 	형 안전한
- [ ] **rebuilt** 	rebuild(다시 세우다)의 과거형
- [ ] **hero** 	명 영웅

Disney

BIG HERO 6

Written by
Laura Hitchcock

Illustrated by
Victoria Ying
Mike Yamada

Designed by
Alfred Giuliani

HIRO and TADASHI

were brothers.

Tadashi invented a **NURSE BOT** named Baymax. A special nursing chip inside Baymax allowed him to help sick people.

Hello. I am Baymax.

Hiro invented tiny machines called MICROBOTS.

Working together, the little microbots could create much larger objects! **Professor Callaghan**, a robotics teacher, was impressed.

After an accident at school, Hiro was
left without his brother. He felt all alone.

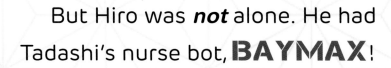

But Hiro was *not* alone. He had
Tadashi's nurse bot, **BAYMAX**!

Hiro and Baymax discovered that a villain named **YOKAI** had *stolen the microbots*!

Yokai sent a swarm of
microbots to attack them.

Hiro's friends
wanted to help . . .

...but **YOKAI** chased them! Hiro and his friends barely *ESCAPED* with their lives!

The team needed a plan to fight Yokai. Hiro invented **high-tech super suits for each of them!**

The suits gave everyone
superpowers!
Even Baymax got a new
suit—with *wings* and
a *rocket fist*!

When Yokai attacked a secret laboratory,
a **DANGEROUS PORTAL** opened up.
It started to pull everything inside!

Then Hiro discovered that Yokai was **PROFESSOR CALLAGHAN**! Callaghan's daughter, Abigail, had been lost when she entered the portal on a risky mission. He wanted *REVENGE* on the scientist who was responsible.

Baymax's sensors were picking up *signs of life*.

HIRO and **BAYMAX** bravely flew into the portal.

They would **RESCUE** Abigail!

Hiro and Baymax found Abigail's lost space pod. But Baymax was damaged and running out of **POWER** fast!

Baymax had a **plan** to get them home.

Hiro hugged
his friend
good-bye.

Then Baymax used the last of his power to **blast his fist** out of the portal, taking Hiro and Abigail with it.

30

Hiro and Abigail were *SAFE*!

But Baymax

was gone.

Even though Hiro had lost Baymax, he
still had the robot's **NURSING CHIP**.
That gave him an **idea**!

Hiro rebuilt Baymax! **BIG HERO 6** was back and ready for action!

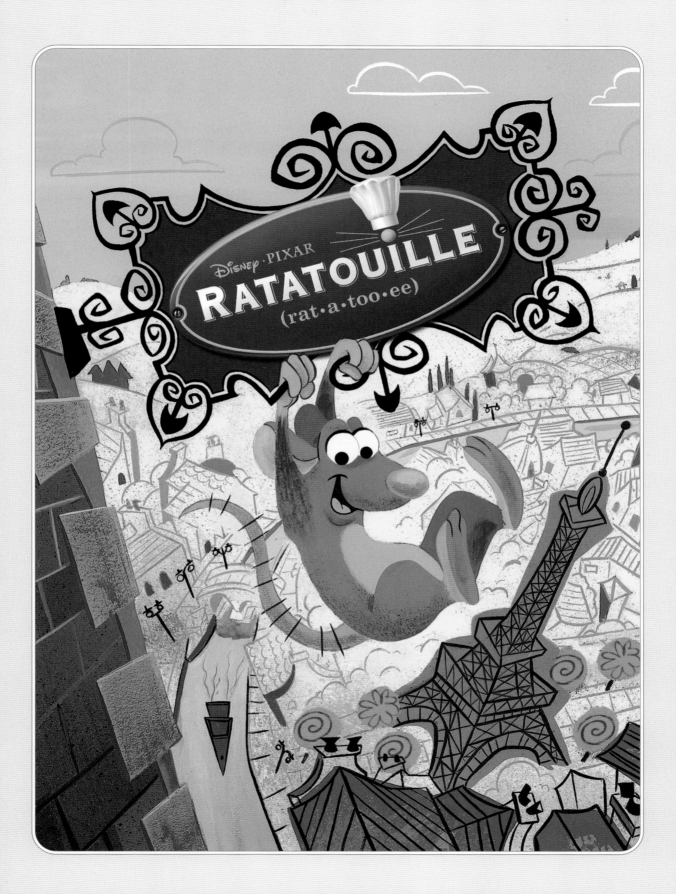

Remy

Linguini

Django

Key Words

☐ rat	몡 쥐	☐ human	몡 사람
☐ dream	몡 꿈 통 꿈꾸다	☐ chase	통 뒤쫓다
☐ extraordinary	혱 뛰어난, 비범한	☐ escape	몡 탈출 통 탈출하다
☐ sense	몡 감각	☐ float	통 떠가다, 뜨다
☐ smell	몡 후각 통 냄새가 나다	☐ separate	통 분리하다, 떼어놓다
☐ chef	몡 요리사	☐ fancy	혱 고급의
☐ poison	몡 독	☐ belong to	~에 속하다
☐ sort	통 분류하다 몡 종류	☐ idol	몡 우상
☐ garbage	몡 쓰레기	☐ pop up	불쑥 나타나다
☐ flee	통 달아나다	☐ imagination	몡 상상

☐ cook	동 요리하다 명 요리사	☐ owner	명 주인
☐ replace	동 교체하다	☐ famous	형 유명한
☐ spill	동 엎지르다, 쏟다	☐ enjoy	동 즐기다
☐ meanwhile	부 그 동안에	☐ attention	명 관심, 주목
☐ find	동 찾다 (find - found - found)	☐ argue	동 다투다
☐ miss	동 그리워하다	☐ guest	명 손님
☐ stay	동 ~한 상태를 유지하다	☐ success	명 성공 동 성공하다
☐ hidden	hide(숨다)의 과거분사	☐ dish	명 요리; 접시
☐ celebrate	동 축하하다	☐ inspector	명 조사관
☐ explain	동 설명하다	☐ proud	형 자랑스러운

Disney · PIXAR

RATATOUILLE
(rat·a·too·ee)

MENU

Written by
Victoria Saxon

Illustrated by
Scott Tilley & Jean-Paul Orpiñas

Designed by
Tony Fejeran

Inspired by the art and character
designs created by Pixar

This is
the story
of Remy,
a little rat
with
BIG
dreams.

Remy wasn't like all the other rats. For one thing, he had an extraordinary sense of

SMELL.

He also had a taste for finer food.

And *THAT* is why Remy dreamed of being . . .

a *CHEF!*

41

But Django,
Remy's father,
had another
job for him . . .

. . . poison checker. The compost heap was where
the rats got all their food. Remy had the
important job of sorting the safe garbage from the
bad garbage. This was NOT part of his dream.

One day,
the rats had to flee
their home. A *HUMAN*
had discovered them!
As the human chased them,
the rats ran to their
ESCAPE boats and
floated into
the sewers.

Remy got separated from the others
and ended up near a fancy French
restaurant—in
PARIS.

The restaurant used to belong to Remy's idol,
the late and great chef, Auguste Gusteau.
Now Gusteau popped up in Remy's

IMAGINATION.

Then—whoops!

Remy fell from
the skylight into
the kitchen.

The restaurant
was an EXCITING place
for Remy, but it was
SCARY, too.

In the kitchen, Remy cooked
a pot of soup to replace what
the garbage boy had spilled.
The garbage boy was
named Linguini. After
that, Linguini and Remy
became friends. *AND*
they were a secret
cooking team.

SHHHH!

Meanwhile, Django and the rest of the rat colony made a new home in the dark, wet sewers under Paris. Things weren't the same without Remy. Django kept hoping he would find his son one day.

But Remy was happy. He did miss his family, but he had found his place in the world. Working together, Linguini and Remy made great food, even though Remy had to stay hidden. The human chefs did not want a rat in their kitchen!

Once, after cooking a wonderful meal, the chefs celebrated in the kitchen. Remy celebrated, too, in the back alley, where . . .

. . . he found his brother EMILE!

Emile took Remy **HOME** to the rats' new colony in the sewer.

52

Of course, Django was HAPPY to see Remy again!

But Remy didn't feel as if he belonged with the rats anymore. He didn't want to go back to smelling garbage.

"I have friends, a place to live, work that I love," Remy tried to explain to his dad. "I'll come back often," he said. But for now he had to return to his new home and the restaurant. Remy's dad didn't understand.

Remy went back to being a little chef. Meanwhile, Linguini was falling in LOVE!

Soon Linguini found out that he was the owner of the restaurant! And the restaurant was becoming very famous. Linguini enjoyed the attention.

55

Linguini decided he didn't need Remy anymore. They **ARGUED.**

Remy felt very
SAD
and
ALONE.

Who was his
family now?

But Linguini needed *HELP*.

He had to cook a special dinner for a special guest. And Linguini told Remy he was SORRY. *UH-OH!* The other chefs didn't like rats, so they left.

Django saw
Linguini being kind
to Remy.
He asked everyone
in the rat colony to
pitch in to help make
the special dinner.
All the rats became
little chefs!

With the rats' help,
the meal was a success.
The SPECIAL dish was
ratatouille!

The rats also helped Remy **CHASE** away the health inspector . . .

. . . who still **CLOSED** the restaurant for having rats.

LA RATATOUILLE

That gave Remy and his friends an idea. They opened a **NEW** one!

And Remy's colony ate at the restaurant, too—enjoying all the fine food they could ever want.

Best of all,
Remy became
a chef at last.

"I am
PROUD
of you
no matter what,"
Django said.

Characters

Riley

Joy

Sadness

Anger

Disgust

Fear

Bing Bong

Key Words

☐ emotion	명 감정	☐ unfair	형 불공평한
☐ mind	명 마음	☐ yucky	형 역겨운
☐ born	bear(태어나다)의 과거분사	☐ proud	형 자랑스러운
☐ charge	명 책임, 담당	☐ memory	명 기억
☐ keep	동 (~한 상태를) 유지하다	☐ core	형 가장 중요한
☐ job	명 일, 직업	☐ power	동 작동시키다
☐ Headquarters	명 본부	☐ personality	명 성격
☐ inside	전 ~의 안에	☐ miss	동 그리워하다; 놓치다
☐ safe	형 안전한	☐ mess	명 엉망인 상태
☐ express	동 표현하다	☐ loose	형 헐거워진, 느슨한

Key Words

☐ turn	통 변하다	☐ forgotten	forget(잊다)의 과거분사
☐ suck	통 빨아들이다	☐ comfort	통 위로하다
☐ lost	lose(잃다)의 과거형, 과거분사	☐ idea	명 생각, 발상
☐ deep	부 깊이 형 깊은	☐ share	통 공유하다, 나누다
☐ positive	형 긍정적인	☐ awful	형 끔찍한
☐ without	전 ~없이	☐ replay	통 재생하다, 되풀이하다
☐ sore	형 화가 난, 감정이 상한	☐ urge	통 ~하도록 설득하다
☐ sulk	통 부루퉁하다	☐ yell	통 소리치다
☐ crumble	통 무너지다	☐ tear	명 눈물
☐ imaginary	형 상상의, 가상적인	☐ adjust	통 ~에 적응하다

Adapted by Andrea Posner-Sanchez
Illustrated by Alan Batson

This is Joy. She is an Emotion who lives in Riley's mind. Ever since Riley was born, Joy has been in charge of keeping her girl happy. Joy is very good at her job!

69

Joy works in Headquarters inside Riley's mind, along with Riley's other Emotions.

Fear helps keep Riley **safe**.

Anger helps Riley express herself if she thinks something is **unfair**—like having to eat broccoli.

Disgust helps Riley stay away from **yucky** things— like broccoli.

And then there is **Sadness**. Joy doesn't understand Sadness. She tries to keep Sadness away from the console—and from Riley's memories.

Joy is proud that most of Riley's memories are happy ones, and she wants to keep them that way!

The most important memories are called **core memories**. They power the **Islands of Personality**—Family Island, Honesty Island, Hockey Island, Friendship Island, and Goofball Island—and make Riley, Riley.

Everything is great until Riley and her family move to a new city. Riley misses her friends, their new house is a mess, and the pizza has **broccoli** on it! Riley's Emotions don't know what to do.

Sadness touches a yellow memory and it turns blue! When Joy tries to stop her, all of Riley's core memories get knocked loose. Joy, Sadness, and all of the core memories get sucked out of Headquarters . . .

. . . and end up lost deep *inside Riley's mind.*

Joy is worried. What will happen to Riley if she's not there to make her happy? Joy tries to stay positive. She tells Sadness they need to get back to Headquarters to return the core memories. That's the only way the Islands of Personality will work again.

Things aren't going well back at Headquarters. Without Joy to run things, the other Emotions have to take charge.

Fear, Anger, and Disgust make Riley act different. She's a sore loser at hockey tryouts.

She talks back to her parents.

At school, she sits alone and **sulks**.

Without her core memories in place, Riley's Islands of Personality begin to **crumble**.

While traveling back to Headquarters, Joy and Sadness run into Riley's old imaginary friend, **Bing Bong**. He is sad because Riley has forgotten him.

Joy is surprised to see that Sadness is able to comfort Bing Bong. Perhaps Sadness is good for something after all.

Meanwhile, Anger gives Riley a terrible idea. She is going to run away!

On their journey, Joy is surprised to find out that she and Sadness share the same favorite memory. It was after a hockey game back in Minnesota. Sadness remembers that Riley missed the winning shot and felt awful.

Joy replays the memory and sees that Riley
was really sad. But then her family and friends
made her feel better. Joy now understands
that sometimes Riley needs to be sad before
she can be happy again.

Joy and Sadness finally make it back to Headquarters.
And they're just in time—Riley is on a bus!
Joy urges Sadness to take over the console.

87

All the Emotions watch as Sadness touches the console.
Riley begins to feel sad right away. She misses her parents.
She yells for the bus driver to stop.

Riley races home. She cries and tells her parents she misses
Minnesota. Her parents say they miss Minnesota, too. Riley
begins to feel better. She smiles through her tears.

Before long, Riley adjusts to her new life in San Francisco. She has new friends, a new hockey team, and all five Emotions working together as a team.

Characters

Rapunzel

Gothel

Flynn

Pascal

Maximus

Key Words

☐ tower	몡 탑	☐ determined	혱 단호한
☐ magical	혱 마법의	☐ hidden	혱 숨겨진 (hide 숨다)
☐ steal	됭 훔치다 (steal-stole-stolen)	☐ person	몡 사람
☐ leave	됭 떠나다	☐ besides	젠 ~외에
☐ light	몡 등불 됭 불을 켜다 (light-lit-lit)	☐ agree	됭 동의하다
☐ float	됭 떠가다, 뜨다	☐ fill	됭 채우다
☐ wish	됭 원하다 몡 소원	☐ escape	됭 탈출하다 몡 탈출
☐ meant	mean(의미하다)의 과거형, 과거분사	☐ glow	됭 빛나다
☐ thief	몡 도둑	☐ jail	몡 감옥
☐ lost	혱 잃어버린	☐ sparkle	됭 반짝거리다

Key Words

- [ ] **come true** 이루어지다
- [ ] **wonderful** 형 아주 멋진, 경이로운
- [ ] **kingdom** 명 왕국
- [ ] **celebrate** 통 기념하다
- [ ] **hold** 통 잡고 있다
- [ ] **shore** 명 해안
- [ ] **return** 통 돌아오다
- [ ] **heartbroken** 형 가슴 아픈
- [ ] **trick** 통 속이다
- [ ] **capture** 통 포획하다

- [ ] **realize** 통 알아차리다, 깨닫다
- [ ] **remember** 통 기억하다
- [ ] **rescue** 통 구출하다 명 구출
- [ ] **hurt** 통 다치게 하다 (hurt-hurt-hurt)
- [ ] **without** 전 ~없이
- [ ] **wither** 통 시들다
- [ ] **evil** 형 사악한
- [ ] **golden** 형 황금빛의
- [ ] **tear** 명 눈물
- [ ] **contain** 통 ~을 포함하다

DISNEP

Tangled

Adapted by
Ben Smiley

Illustrated by
Victoria Ying

Rapunzel had long, long hair and lived in a tall, tall tower. Her hair was as long as the tower was tall. When Mother Gothel came home every day, she called, **"Rapunzel, let down your hair!"** And Rapunzel pulled Mother Gothel up into the tower.

Rapunzel's hair was **magical**. It kept Mother Gothel young and beautiful.

Rapunzel did not know that Mother Gothel had stolen her from her real parents, the King and the Queen.

Mother Gothel wanted the **magical** hair all for herself.

Mother Gothel never let Rapunzel leave the tower. She told Rapunzel that bad people wanted to take her **magical** hair. Rapunzel had one friend—a chameleon named **Pascal**.

Once a year, on her birthday, Rapunzel saw **sparkling lights** floating into the sky. She wished she could leave the tower and see the lights up close. They seemed **meant** for her.

One day, just before Rapunzel's eighteenth birthday, a thief named **Flynn** was running through the forest. He had stolen the lost princess's crown. While trying to get away from Maximus, a determined horse from the royal guard, Flynn found Rapunzel's hidden tower.

Flynn climbed up the tower to hide. Rapunzel had never seen another person besides Mother Gothel. Rapunzel thought Flynn wanted her hair. But he didn't. Rapunzel showed Flynn a painting she had made of the **lights** and asked him to take her to see them. Flynn agreed.

On the way, Flynn and Rapunzel stopped in a pub. It was filled with scary-looking men. But they didn't want to steal Rapunzel's hair, either. They were **friendly**.

Maximus and some royal guards found Flynn. One of the scary-looking men helped Flynn and Rapunzel escape.

They ran until they got trapped in a water-filled cave. Rapunzel's magical **glowing** hair helped them find a way out!

But Maximus found Flynn again. The horse wanted to take Flynn to jail. Rapunzel told **Maximus** it was her birthday. She asked him to let Flynn take her to see the sparkling lights. Maximus agreed. Rapunzel's wish was about to come true!

Flynn and Rapunzel had a **wonderful** day. A little boy gave Rapunzel a small kingdom flag. The kingdom was celebrating the birthday of the lost princess.

The lost princess had the same birthday as Rapunzel!

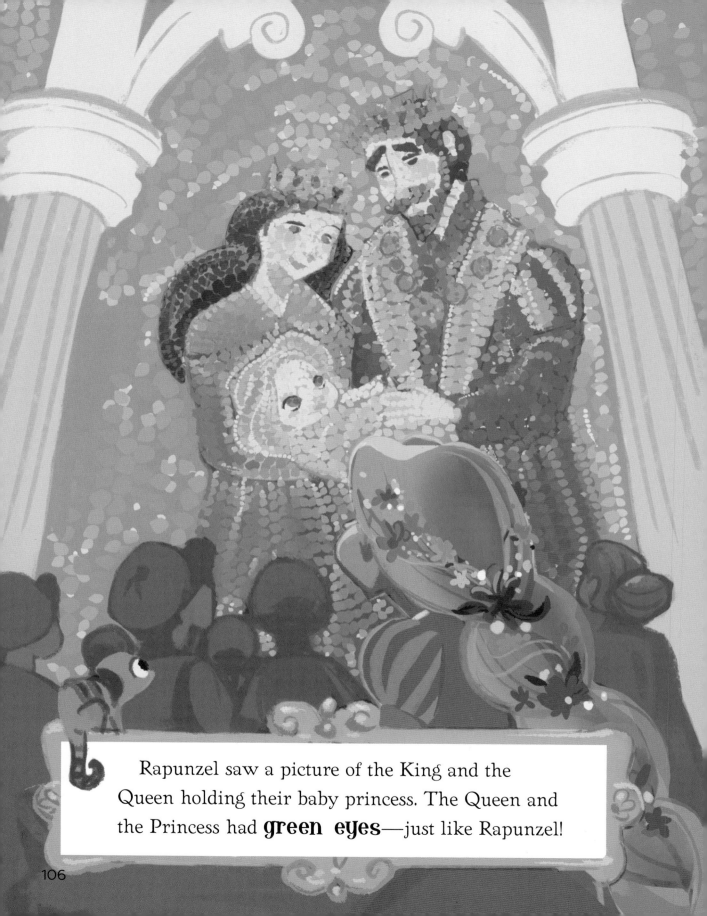

Rapunzel saw a picture of the King and the
Queen holding their baby princess. The Queen and
the Princess had **green eyes**—just like Rapunzel!

Suddenly, Rapunzel was swept up in a dance! It was the most **fun** she had ever had . . . so far.

That night, the people of the kingdom lit lanterns.
At last, Rapunzel's wish came true. Overjoyed, she saw the
sparkling lights fill the sky. She loved the world outside
the tower. She loved Flynn. And he loved her, too.

On shore, Flynn left Rapunzel and did not return. Rapunzel was **heartbroken**. She did not know that Flynn had been tricked by evil Mother Gothel. He had been captured and put in jail! Mother Gothel found Rapunzel and took her back to the tower.

Back in her room, Rapunzel realized that she had been painting the kingdom's emblem, the **golden sun**, on her wall her entire life!

Rapunzel remembered the picture of the **lost princess** and the Queen. Now Rapunzel knew why they all looked alike.

Mother Gothel was the only one who wanted to steal Rapunzel's **magical** hair. She had lied to Rapunzel about everything. **"Mother, I am the lost princess,"** Rapunzel said.

Meanwhile, Flynn had escaped and arrived at the tower to rescue Rapunzel.

"Rapunzel! Rapunzel! Let down your hair!" he called.

But Mother Gothel would not let Rapunzel go. Mother Gothel hurt Flynn so badly that he could never, ever take Rapunzel from her.

Flynn still thought of a way to save Rapunzel. He **cut** her hair. Without Rapunzel's magical hair, Mother Gothel withered away. Rapunzel was finally free of the evil woman.

But without her long hair, Rapunzel had no more magic to save Flynn. He closed his eyes for the last time.

Rapunzel cried. A single **golden tear** fell on Flynn's cheek. It contained the last bit of magic left inside Rapunzel. Flynn's eyes opened! He was all right!

Rapunzel went to her real parents, the King and the Queen. After eighteen years of waiting, they took one look at the **green-eyed** girl and knew she was their daughter. Rapunzel had come home at last!

Rapunzel loved her new life. She loved the world outside the tower. She loved her new friends. At last, she knew where she belonged.

And they all lived **happily** ever after.

Characters

Woody

Forky

Buzz

Bo Peep

Bonnie

Gabby Gabby

Key Words

☐ sheriff	명 보안관	☐ catch	동 잡다
☐ leader	명 지도자, 대표	☐ antique	명 골동품 형 골동품인
☐ toy	명 장난감	☐ instead	부 대신에
☐ hand	명 도움	☐ seem	동 ~인 것 같다
☐ change	동 변하다, 바뀌다	☐ friendly	형 친절한
☐ orientation	명 예비소집	☐ capture	동 붙잡다
☐ nervous	형 불안한	☐ escape	동 탈출하다
☐ imagination	명 상상력	☐ familiar	형 익숙한, 친숙한
☐ life	명 삶, 생명	☐ rescue	동 구출하다 명 구출
☐ leave	동 떠나다	☐ brave	형 용감한

Key Words

- [ ] search   통 찾다
- [ ] trail   명 흔적
- [ ] free   통 풀어 주다
- [ ] sneak   통 살금살금 가다
- [ ] roam   통 돌아다니다
- [ ] aisle   명 복도
- [ ] cabinet   명 캐비닛, 보관장
- [ ] stray   형 길을 잃은, 주인이 없는
- [ ] leap   통 뛰어오르다
- [ ] spot   통 발견하다

- [ ] chase   통 뒤쫓다
- [ ] deal   명 거래
- [ ] exchange   명 교환
- [ ] reach   통 ~에 닿다, 이르다
- [ ] string   명 끈
- [ ] soar   통 날아오르다
- [ ] perfect   형 완벽한
- [ ] thrilled   형 신이 난
- [ ] reunite   통 재회하다
- [ ] accomplish   통 해내다, 성취하다

Adapted by
Josh Crute

Illustrated by
Matt Kaufenberg

Designed by
Tony Fejeran

Howdy, partner! Meet Woody, the sheriff round these parts. Woody loved his kid, Andy, and was the leader of the toys in Andy's room. But sometimes he needed help. Thankfully, his best friend, Bo Peep, was always there to lend a hand.

Then one day, **everything changed**.

Bo Peep was getting a new kid—and
Woody was **staying behind**.

Years later, Woody got a new kid, too. Her name was **Bonnie**. At **kindergarten orientation**, she was a little nervous.

Luckily, she had a sheriff around! When
a boy took her art supplies, Woody rustled
them up, along with some new ones. Bonnie
used her **imagination** to put them together
to make a new friend. . . .

Forky!

To Woody's surprise, Forky **came to life**—just like the other toys!

Forky was surprised, too. He didn't think he was a toy at all—he was a spork! So when Bonnie's family went on a road trip in their RV . . .

Forky made a break for it!

Sheriff Woody would never leave anyone behind. He jumped out the window after Forky.

Woody took Forky to the next town to catch up with Bonnie. Then something in the window of an antiques store caught his eye . . . **Bo's lamp!**

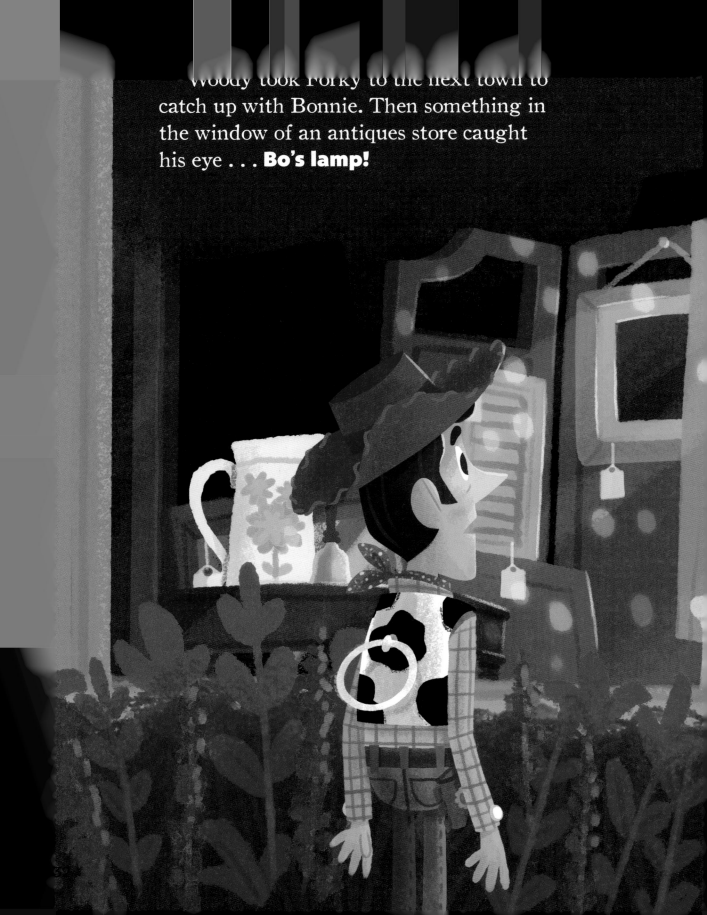

Woody and Forky went into the store. Instead of finding Bo, they saw a doll named **Gabby Gabby**. She seemed friendly at first—but then she said she wanted Woody's voice box. She told her team to capture Woody and Forky!

Woody escaped to a nearby playground, where he saw a familiar face—**Bo Peep!** She and her tiny friend, **Giggle McDimples**, were traveling with a group of toys to find kids to play with. Bo said she would help Woody rescue Forky!

Meanwhile, **Buzz Lightyear** was searching for Woody and Forky. The brave space ranger followed their trail to a carnival, but he got stuck to a prize wall. He met a couple of toys, **Ducky and Bunny**. Buzz accidentally set both of them free!

Buzz found Woody and Bo, and the whole group sneaked into the antiques store. Forky was trapped in a **tall cabinet**.

The store's cat, **Dragon**, roamed the aisles, looking for stray toys to gobble up. The friends had to figure out a plan.

Bo found **Duke Caboom**, Canada's greatest stuntman. He would help rescue Forky, as well as Bo's sheep. They had been captured, too.

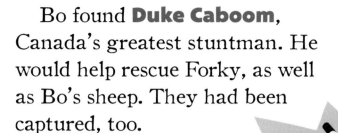

Duke leaped across the aisle to the cabinet. **But he didn't make it.** Dragon spotted him and the toys!

Bo found her sheep just as Dragon began to **chase** Duke. The toys held on tight!

They made it out of the store—but Forky was still inside. Most of the group was too **tired and scared** to try a new plan. They decided to leave.

But Woody needed to get Forky. He made a deal with Gabby Gabby. In exchange for Forky, he gave her his **voice box**. And he would take her to Bonnie so she could have a kid, too.

The toys returned to help Woody and Gabby Gabby. But there was only **one way** to reach Bonnie. They went to the carnival and rode to the top of the Ferris wheel. Then they tied a long string around Duke's bike.

Duke took a deep breath, **revved his engine** . . .

. . . and **SOARED** over the crowd!

Thanks to Duke, the toys zipped across the carnival on the string. Then Gabby Gabby noticed a girl who was lost and needed a friend. Gabby Gabby was perfect for her! The girl hugged the doll close just before she found her parents. **Gabby Gabby got a kid!**

The toys found Bonnie. She was **thrilled** to see Forky again!

Woody loved seeing the two of them **so happy**.

And he was glad to be **reunited** with his friends.

Woody realized that lost and lonely toys
were everywhere, and he wanted to help them.
He knew with Bo and their friends, he could
accomplish anything!

Disney · PIXAR
Story Collection 1

Activity Book

CONTENTS

★북 퀴즈
스토리를 읽고 나서 얼마나 정확히 이해했는지 북 퀴즈를 통해 이해도를 테스트합니다.
스토리의 중심 주제와 세부사항에 관한 문제로,
맞힌 개수에 따라 자신의 독해력을 확인할 수 있어요.

★학습 액티비티
어휘력과 독해력을 길러주는 다양한 문제 액티비티가 수록되었습니다.
또한 이야기 전반을 다시 이해하며 글의 구조를 정리하는 연습을 합니다.

Name: _____   **Date:** _____ / _____ / _____

1. What did Hiro and Tadashi love to do?

   ① to create large objects
   ② to create new inventions
   ③ to invent high-tech super suits
   ④ to invent dangerous portals

2. What did Hiro invent?

   ① microbots
   ② a dangerous portal
   ③ a nurse bot
   ④ a secret laboratory

3. What is the name of Tadashi's nurse bot?

   ① Yokai   ② Callaghan
   ③ Abigail   ④ Baymax

4. After a/an _____ at school, Hiro was left without his brother.

   ① mission   ② accident
   ③ action   ④ mistake

5. What did the villain steal?

   ① the microbots
   ② a special nursing chip
   ③ super wings
   ④ high-tech super suits

6. When Yokai chased them, Hiro and his friends barely _____ with their lives.

   ① invented   ② escaped
   ③ needed   ④ attacked

7. What did Baymax's new suit have?

   ① robotics
   ② special nursing chips
   ③ large objects
   ④ wings and a rocket fist

8. Who was the villain?

   ① Tadashi   ② Hiro
   ③ Professor Callaghan ④ the microbots

3

9. What happened when Yokai attacked a secret laboratory?

　① His daughter was lost.
　② Hiro discovered that Yokai stole his nurse bot.
　③ Hiro planned to fight Yokai.
　④ A dangerous portal opened up.

10. Abigail had been lost when she entered the _____ on a risky mission.

　① school　　　② portal
　③ laboratory　④ sensors

11. Callaghan wanted _____ on the scientist who was responsible.

　① invention　② mission
　③ revenge　　④ microbots

12. What did Baymax's sensors pick up from the portal?

　① superpowers
　② Hiro's action
　③ Tadashi's nurse bot
　④ signs of life

13. What did Hiro and Baymax find?

　① Abigail's space pod
　② Baymax's rocket fist
　③ Tadashi's special chips
　④ Yokai's high-tech super suits

14. Baymax was damaged and running out of _____ fast.

　① chips　　② power
　③ object　④ suits

15. What did Hiro do at the end of the story?

　① He rebuilt Baymax.
　② He lost his microbots.
　③ He invented high-tech super suits.
　④ He flew into the portal.

Score: _____ / 15

• Score 11~15: 이야기를 읽고 세부 내용을 잘 파악하고 있어요.

• Score 6~10: 이야기의 전체적인 흐름을 대체로 잘 파악하고 있어요.

• Score 0~5: 단어 학습을 한 후, 이야기를 다시 한번 읽어 보세요.

BOOK QUIZ
Ratatouille

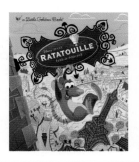

Name: _____   **Date:** _____ / _____ / _____

1. What did Remy dream of becoming?

   ① a chef
   ② a police officer
   ③ a teacher
   ④ a doctor

2. Why did the rats have to flee their home?

   ① Some dogs found them.
   ② A human discovered them.
   ③ There was an earthquake.
   ④ A cat discovered them.

3. Where did Remy end up after being separated from the others?

   ① Paris   ② New York
   ③ Rome   ④ California

4. What is the name of the garbage boy in the kitchen?

   ① Auguste   ② Django
   ③ Linguini   ④ Emile

5. Remy and Linguini became friends, and they were a secret _____ team.

   ① baking   ② sewing
   ③ dancing   ④ cooking

6. Who did Remy find in the back alley?

   ① his father
   ② his uncle
   ③ his brother
   ④ his sister

7. How did Remy feel when he went back to the sewer?

   ① He was sad to see his father.
   ② He liked the smelly garbage.
   ③ He didn't feel as if he belonged with the rats.
   ④ He wanted to stay forever.

8. Linguini found out that he was the _____ of the restaurant.

   ① owner   ② inspector
   ③ manager   ④ janitor

9. What happened when Linguini didn't need Remy anymore?

   ① They apologized.
   ② They hugged.
   ③ They cried.
   ④ They argued.

10. Who did Linguini have to cook a special dinner for?

   ① his mother
   ② his father
   ③ a special guest
   ④ a king

11. Why did the other chefs leave when Remy came back?

   ① They didn't like rats.
   ② They thought rats were smart.
   ③ They wanted to get a better job.
   ④ They needed to rest.

12. Who saw Linguini being kind to Remy?

   ① Django   ② Emile
   ③ the special guest   ④ the other chefs

13. What was the special dish that the rats made?

   ① cream pasta   ② ratatouille
   ③ mushroom soup ④ steak

14. The rats also helped Remy chase away the _____.

   ① head chef   ② special guest
   ③ health inspector ④ new owner

15. What did Remy and his friends do in the end?

   ① They went back to the sewer.
   ② They opened a new restaurant.
   ③ They went on a vacation.
   ④ They built a new home.

Score: _____ / 15

• Score 11~15: 이야기를 읽고 세부 내용을 잘 파악하고 있어요.

• Score 6~10: 이야기의 전체적인 흐름을 대체로 잘 파악하고 있어요.

• Score 0~5: 단어 학습을 한 후, 이야기를 다시 한번 읽어 보세요.

Name: _____ **Date:** _____ / _____ / _____

1. Where does Joy live?

   ① in Riley's mind
   ② in Heather's mind
   ③ in Jacob's mind
   ④ in Simon's mind

2. What is Joy in charge of?

   ① making Riley sad
   ② keeping Riley happy
   ③ helping Riley walk
   ④ making Riley cry

3. Who helps keep Riley safe?

   ① Anger   ② Sadness
   ③ Fear   ④ Disgust

4. What are the most important memories called?

   ① right memories   ② core memories
   ③ front memories   ④ side memories

5. Everything is great until Riley and her family move to _____.

   ① a new country
   ② a new city
   ③ a new village
   ④ a new building

6. What color did a yellow memory turn when Sadness touched it?

   ① blue   ② green
   ③ purple   ④ pink

7. Where did Joy and Sadness have to go to return the core memories?

   ① Headquarters
   ② Family Island
   ③ Dark pit
   ④ Riley's old city

8. Who took charge of Headquarters while Joy was gone?

① Sadness
② Fear, Disgust, and Anger
③ Jumbo
④ Love

9. How did Fear, Anger, and Disgust make Riley act?

① different   ② the same
③ special   ④ kind

10. What began to crumble away?

① Riley's Islands of Relationships
② Riley's Islands of Friendships
③ Riley's Islands of Personality
④ Riley's Islands of Kindness

11. Who was Riley's imaginary friend?

① Jack   ② Peggy
③ Doug   ④ Bing Bong

12. What terrible idea did Anger give Riley?

① to quit school
② to run away
③ to yell at her teacher
④ to hit her sister

13. Riley's family and _____ made her feel better when she was sad.

① friends   ② neighbors
③ teachers   ④ pets

14. Who does Joy urge to take over the console?

① Sadness   ② Anger
③ Fear   ④ Disgust

15. What did Riley tell her parents that she missed?

① her core memories
② Bing Bong
③ Minnesota
④ the Emotions

Score: _____ / 15

• Score 11~15: 이야기를 읽고 세부 내용을 잘 파악하고 있어요.

• Score 6~10: 이야기의 전체적인 흐름을 대체로 잘 파악하고 있어요.

• Score 0~5: 단어 학습을 한 후, 이야기를 다시 한번 읽어 보세요.

BOOK QUIZ
Tangled

Name: _____

1. What kind of hair did Rapunzel have?

   ① long hair   ② short hair
   ③ green hair   ④ blue hair

2. Who asked Rapunzel to let down her hair every day?

   ① the King
   ② the Queen
   ③ Mother Gothel
   ④ her friend

3. Rapunzel's hair kept Mother Gothel young and _____.

   ① sad   ② healthy
   ③ beautiful   ④ ugly

4. Who were Rapunzel's real parents?

   ① the Prince and the Princess
   ② the King and the Queen
   ③ the poor farmers
   ④ the servants of the castle

5. What was the name of Rapunzel's chameleon friend?

   ① Terry   ② Pascal
   ③ James   ④ Anne

6. Every year, Rapunzel saw _____ lights floating into the sky.

   ① sparkling   ② red
   ③ pink   ④ green

7. What did a thief named Flynn steal?

   ① the lost princess's crown
   ② the lost princess's shoe
   ③ the lost princess's ring
   ④ the lost princess's ribbon

8. Why did Flynn climb up the tower?

   ① He had to hide.
   ② He had to pray.
   ③ He had to sleep.
   ④ He had to eat.

9. The scary-looking men in the pub were
   _____.

   ① rude
   ② mean
   ③ loud
   ④ friendly

10. Maximus and some royal _____
    found Flynn.

    ① guards
    ② doctors
    ③ maids
    ④ chefs

11. What was the color of the Queen and
    the Princess's eyes?

    ① blue
    ② brown
    ③ black
    ④ green

12. Why was Rapunzel heartbroken?

    ① Flynn did not return.
    ② Flynn cut her hair.
    ③ Flynn stole the crown.
    ④ Flynn helped her escape.

13. Where did Mother Gothel take
    Rapunzel when she found her?

    ① to the castle
    ② to the ship
    ③ to the tower
    ④ to the wagon

14. What did Mother Gothel do to Flynn?

    ① She made him run away.
    ② She hurt him badly.
    ③ She turned him into a frog.
    ④ She cut his hair.

15. A single _____ tear fell on Flynn's
    cheek.

    ① golden   ② silver
    ③ purple   ④ pink

Score: _____ / 15

• Score 11~15: 이야기를 읽고 세부 내용을 잘 파악하고 있어요.

• Score 6~10: 이야기의 전체적인 흐름을 대체로 잘 파악하고 있어요.

• Score 0~5: 단어 학습을 한 후, 이야기를 다시 한번 읽어 보세요.

Name: _____ **Date:** _____ / _____ / _____

1. Who was the leader of the toys in Andy's room?

   ① Bo Peep   ② Woody
   ③ Buzz   ④ Potato

2. How did Bonnie feel at kindergarten orientation?

   ① excited   ② tired
   ③ nervous   ④ happy

3. What did Bonnie make using her imagination?

   ① Forky   ② Spoony
   ③ Knifey   ④ Choppy

4. What caught Woody's eye in the window of an antiques store?

   ① Bo's cane   ② Bo's hat
   ③ Bo's skirt   ④ Bo's lamp

5. Gabby Gabby seemed _____ at first.

   ① friendly   ② charming
   ③ rude   ④ scary

6. Where did Woody see Bo Peep?

   ① at a cafeteria
   ② at a library
   ③ at a playground
   ④ at a candy store

7. Who was searching for Woody and Forky?

   ① Ducky   ② Buzz Lightyear
   ③ Giggle   ④ Cathy

8. Forky was trapped in a tall _____ in the antiques store.

   ① cabinet   ② drawer
   ③ tumbler   ④ box

11

9. Who was Dragon?

① the store's dog
② the store's hamster
③ the store's cat
④ the store's bird

10. Duke Caboom was Canada's greatest
_____.

① hockey player
② stuntman
③ actor
④ singer

11. Why did the group decide to leave
after they got out of the store?

① They were too tired and scared.
② They were hungry.
③ They wanted to play.
④ They needed to go back home.

12. Where did the toys go to reach Bonnie?

① the carnival
② the hospital
③ the school
④ the playground

13. Bonnie was _____ to see Forky
again.

① disappointed
② mad
③ annoyed
④ thrilled

14. Why was Woody glad at the end of the
story?

① He reunited with his friends.
② He went back to Andy.
③ He got a new kid.
④ He met his parents.

15. Woody wanted to help lost and lonely
_____.

① animals   ② kids
③ pets   ④ toys

Score: _____ / 15

• Score 11~15: 이야기를 읽고 세부 내용을 잘 파악하고 있어요.

• Score 6~10: 이야기의 전체적인 흐름을 대체로 잘 파악하고 있어요.

• Score 0~5: 단어 학습을 한 후, 이야기를 다시 한번 읽어 보세요.

Activities

WORD Check

A 다음 단어의 알맞은 우리말 뜻에 동그라미 하세요.

① invention (발명품 / 기계)

② accident (사고 / 발견)

③ create (도착하다 / 창조하다)

④ escape (발명하다 / 탈출하다)

⑤ nurse (간호사 / 변호사)

⑥ suit (옷 / 못)

⑦ machine (기차 / 기계)

⑧ rescue (공격하다 / 구출하다)

B 빈칸에 알맞은 단어를 써 넣어 퍼즐을 완성하세요.

Across	① 임무	② 공격하다	③ 영웅
Down	④ 주먹	⑤ 위험한	⑥ 발견하다

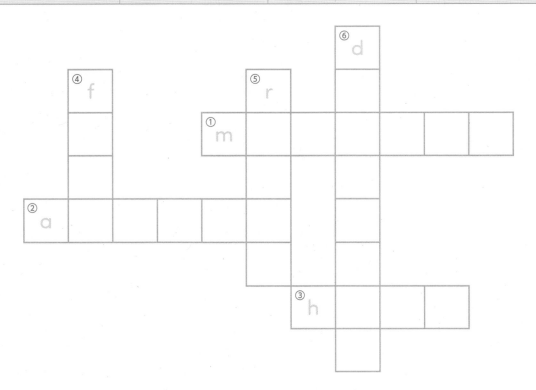

14

C 다음 단어를 사용하여 문장을 완성하세요.

blast	plan	revenge
name	safe	secret

1 When Yokai attacked a _____ laboratory, a dangerous portal opened up.

2 Professor Callaghan wanted _____ on the scientist who was responsible.

3 Tadashi invented a nurse bot _____d Baymax.

4 Baymax had a _____ to get them home. Hiro hugged his friend good-bye.

5 Baymax used the last of his power to _____ his fist out of the portal, taking Hiro and Abigail with it.

6 Hiro and Abigail were _____! But Baymax was gone.

A 등장인물에 어울리는 단어를 골라 쓰세요.

brothers   father   daughter   friends   a nurse bot

Character Map

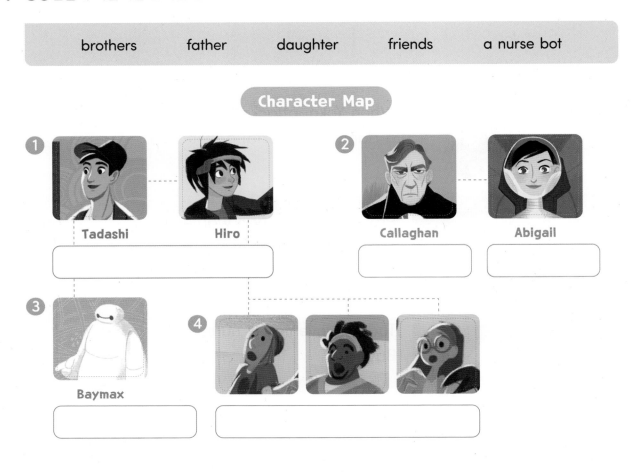

B 이야기와 일치하는 문장에는 T, 일치하지 않는 문장에는 F에 동그라미 하세요.

① Baymax could create much larger objects.　　　　T　F

② Hiro and Baymax discovered that Yokai had stolen the microbots.　　　　T　F

③ Hiro discovered that Yokai was Professor Callaghan.　　　　T　F

④ Hiro had lost Baymax's nursing chip.　　　　T　F

C 다음 글에 알맞은 그림을 찾아 연결하세요.

1 Hiro and Tadashi loved to create fantastic new inventions.

2 Hiro was not alone. He had Tadashi's nurse bot, Baymax!

3 Yokai chased Hiro and his friends. They barely escaped with their lives.

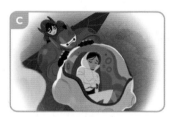

4 When Yokai attacked a secret laboratory, a dangerous portal opened up.

5 Hiro and Baymax found Abigail's lost space pod.

6 Even though Hiro had lost Baymax, he still had the robot's nursing chip.

A 알맞은 단어에 동그라미 하여 문장을 완성하세요.

1 A special nursing [chip / pod] inside Baymax allowed him to help sick people.

2 Hiro and Baymax discovered that a villain named Yokai had [borrowed / stolen] the microbots.

3 Hiro invented high-tech [tiny / super] suits for each of them.

4 Then Hiro [discovered / disagreed] that Yokai was Professor Callaghan.

5 Even Baymax got a new suit with wings and a rocket [fist / tail].

6 Abigail had been [safe / lost] when she entered the portal on a risky mission.

7 Baymax's sensors were picking up signs of [life / power].

8 Hiro and Baymax bravely [swam / flew] into the portal.

9 Even though Hiro had lost Baymax, he still had the robot's [nursing / chasing] chip.

10 Big [Hero / Villain] 6 was back and ready for action.

B 다음 단어들을 이용해 우리말 뜻에 맞는 문장을 완성하세요.

1

| brothers | were | Hiro and Tadashi | . |

히로와 타다시는 형제였어요.

→ _____

2

| invented | tiny | Hiro | called | machines | microbots | . |

히로는 마이크로봇이라고 불리는 아주 작은 기계를 발명했어요.

→ _____

3

| the team | a plan | to fight | Yokai | needed | . |

팀은 요카이와 싸우기 위해 계획이 필요했어요.

→ _____

4

| gave | the suits | everyone | superpowers | . |

그 옷들은 모두에게 강력한 힘을 주었어요.

→ _____

5

| would | Abigail | rescue | they | . |

그들은 에비게일을 구출할 거예요.

→ _____

6

| safe | Hiro and Abigail | were | . |

히로와 에비게일은 무사했어요.

→ _____

문장의 빈칸을 채워 이야기의 구조를 한눈에 정리해 보세요.

space	laboratory	attack	safe	revenge	mission

Cause

Callaghan's daughter, Abigail, had been lost when she entered the portal on a risky ① _____.
He wanted ② _____ on the scientist who was responsible.

Effect

Yokai, Professor Callaghan, stole Hiro's microbots.
He sent a swarm of microbots to ③ _____ Hiro and his friends.
Finally, he attacked a secret ④ _____.

Result

Hiro and Baymax found Abigail's lost ⑤ _____ pod.
Baymax blasted his fist out of the portal, taking Hiro and Abigail with it.
Hiro and Abigail were ⑥ _____.

Activities

A 다음 단어의 알맞은 우리말 뜻에 동그라미 하세요.

1 dream (잠 / 꿈)

2 imagination (현실 / 상상)

3 human (인간 / 사물)

4 celebrate (축하하다 / 저주하다)

5 escape (붙잡힘 / 탈출)

6 explain (설명하다 / 무시하다)

7 fancy (저렴한 / 고급의)

8 inspector (용의자 / 조사관)

B 빈칸에 알맞은 단어를 써 넣어 퍼즐을 완성하세요.

Across	① 쓰레기	② 요리사	③ 머무르다
Down	④ 손님	⑤ 요리; 접시	⑥ 즐기다

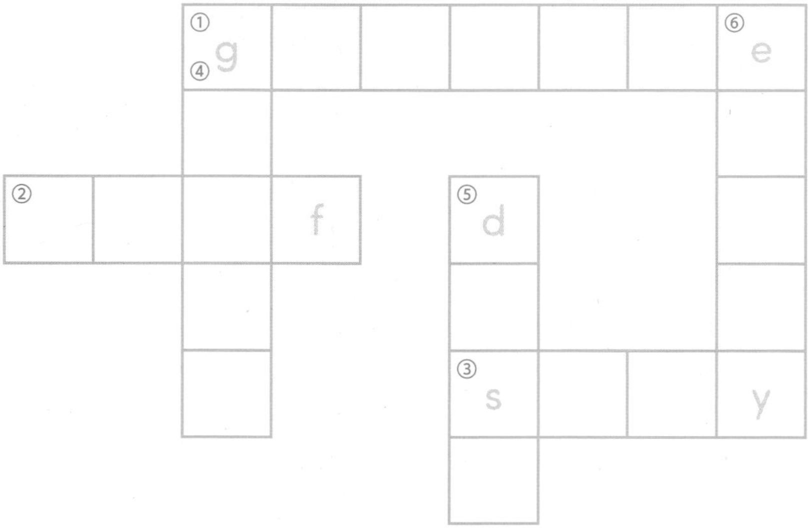

C 다음 단어를 사용하여 문장을 완성하세요.

| famous | proud | cook | sense | sorting | success |

1 For one thing, Remy had an extraordinary _____ of smell.

2 In the kitchen, Remy _____ed a pot of soup to replace what the garbage boy had spilled.

3 Linguini and the restaurant were becoming very _____!

4 Remy had the important job of _____ the safe garbage from the bad garbage.

5 With the rats' help, the meal was a _____.

6 "I am so _____ of you no matter what," Django said.

STORY Check

A 빈칸을 채워 Linguini의 문제가 어떻게 해결되었는지 정리해 보세요.

success	rats	dinner	special

Problem

Linguini had to cook a special ① _____ for a special guest.
But the other chefs didn't like ② _____, so they left.

→

Solution

Django asked everyone in the rat colony to pitch in to help make the special dinner.
With the rats' help, the meal was a ③ _____.
The ④ _____ dish was ratatouille!

B 아래 문장을 읽고 이유에 따른 결과를 찾아 기호를 써보세요.

Cause: Why It Happened

❶ A human discovered Remy's family and chased them. ⟶ ☐

❷ Remy had an extraordinary sense of smell.
He also had a taste for finer food. ⟶ ☐

❸ The human chefs did not want a rat in their kitchen. ⟶ ☐

Effect: What Happened

ⓐ Remy dreamed of being a chef.

ⓑ The rats ran to their escape boats and floated into the sewers.

ⓒ Remy had to stay hidden.

24

C 다음 글에 알맞은 그림을 찾아 연결하세요.

1 Django kept hoping he would find his son one day.

2 Django was happy to see Remy again.

3 Remy went back to being a little chef. Meanwhile, Linguini was falling in love.

4 Linguini decided he didn't need Remy anymore. They argued.

5 The rats helped Remy chase away the health inspector, who still closed the restaurant for having rats.

6 Remy's colony ate at the restaurant, enjoying all the fine food they could ever want.

A 알맞은 단어에 동그라미 하여 문장을 완성하세요.

① This is the story of Remy, a little rat with big ⎡ menus / dreams ⎤ .

② He also had a taste for finer ⎡ food / clothes ⎤ .

③ The restaurant was an exciting place for Remy, but it was ⎡ hard / scary ⎤ , too.

④ After cooking a wonderful ⎡ pudding / meal ⎤ , the chefs celebrated in the kitchen.

⑤ Emile took Remy home to the rats' new colony in the ⎡ sewer / restaurant ⎤ .

⑥ Remy didn't want to go back to smelling ⎡ kitchens / garbage ⎤ .

⑦ Linguini decided he didn't need Remy anymore. Remy felt very sad and ⎡ alone / afraid ⎤ .

⑧ Linguini had to cook a special dinner for a special ⎡ guest / friend ⎤ .

⑨ The ⎡ chefs / rats ⎤ also helped Remy chase away the health inspector.

⑩ Remy's colony ate at the restaurant, enjoying all the fine food they could ever ⎡ want / draw ⎤ .

26

B 다음 단어들을 이용해 우리말 뜻에 맞는 문장을 완성하세요.

1

| all the other rats | wasn't | Remy | like | . |

레미는 다른 쥐들과 같지 않았어요.

→ _____

2

| into the kitchen | from the skylight | fell | Remy | . |

레미는 채광창에서 주방 안으로 떨어졌어요.

→ _____

3

| didn't want | to smelling garbage | to go back | Remy | . |

레미는 냄새 나는 쓰레기로 돌아가고 싶지 않았어요.

→ _____

4

| they | the other chefs | so | didn't like rats, | left | . |

다른 요리사들은 쥐를 싫어했기 때문에 떠났어요.

→ _____

5

| became | little | all the rats | chefs | ! |

모든 쥐들은 작은 요리사가 되었어요!

→ _____

6

| became | at last | Remy | best of all, | a chef | . |

무엇보다도, 레미는 마침내 요리사가 되었어요.

→ _____

STORY MAP

문장의 빈칸을 채워 이야기의 구조를 한눈에 정리해 보세요.

| success | restaurant | secret | need | friends | owner | guest | sorry |

Beginning

Remy got separated from his family and ended up near a fancy French ① _____ in Paris.

Middle

In the kitchen, Remy cooked a pot of soup to replace what the garbage boy, Linguini, had spilled. After that, Linguini and Remy became ② _____. They were a ③ _____ cooking team.

Linguini became the ④ _____ of the restaurant. The restaurant was becoming very famous. Linguini decided he didn't ⑤ _____ Remy anymore. They argued.

Linguini had to cook a special dinner for a special ⑥ _____.
Linguini told Remy he was ⑦ _____.
But the other chefs didn't like rats, so they left.

End

Remy and his family helped make the special dinner. With the rats' help, the meal was a ⑧ _____. The special dish was ratatouille!

28

DISNEY·PIXAR
INSIDE OUT

Activities

A 다음 단어의 알맞은 우리말 뜻에 동그라미 하세요.

1 job (일 / 상대)

2 tear (눈물 / 여행)

3 imaginary (사나운 / 상상의)

4 safe (안전한 / 사악한)

5 personality (성격 / 행동)

6 positive (자랑스러운 / 긍정적인)

7 yell (소리치다 / 속삭이다)

8 memory (기억 / 용기)

B 빈칸에 알맞은 단어를 써 넣어 퍼즐을 완성하세요.

Across	① 역겨운	② 생각	③ 적응하다
Down	④ 마음	⑤ 재생하다	⑥ 부루퉁하다

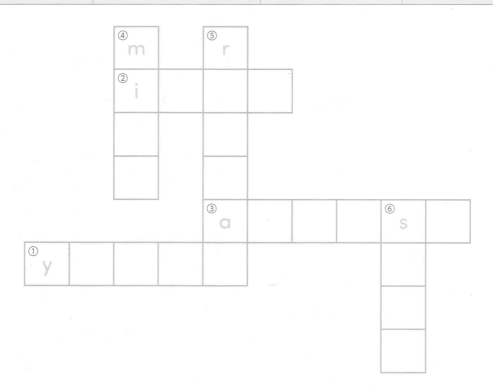

C 다음 단어를 사용하여 문장을 완성하세요.

| core | unfair | share | urge | comfort | crumble |

① Anger helps Riley express herself if she thinks something is _____ — like having to eat broccoli.

② The most important memories are called _____ memories.

③ Without her core memories in place, Riley's Islands of Personality begin to _____ away!

④ Joy is surprised to see that Sadness is able to _____ Bing Bong.

⑤ On their journey, Joy is surprised to find out that she and Sadness _____ the same favorite memory.

⑥ Joy _____s Sadness to take over the console.

A Emotion(감정)들의 이름을 완성하고 각각 어떤 일을 하는지 맞게 연결해 보세요.

①  A_____ •

②  S_____ •

③  D_____ •

④  J_____ •

⑤  F_____ •

ⓐ He helps keep Riley safe.

ⓑ She helps Riley stay away from yucky things.

ⓒ He helps Riley express herself if she thinks something is unfair.

ⓓ She keeps Riley happy.

ⓔ She is able to comfort Riley.

B 이야기와 일치하는 문장에는 T, 일치하지 않는 문장에는 F에 동그라미 하세요.

① Joy works in Headquarters inside Riley's mind.   T   F

② The most important memories are called Headquarters.   T   F

③ Riley and her family move to a new city.   T   F

④ Sadness is able to comfort Bing Bong.   T   F

C 다음 글에 알맞은 그림을 찾아 연결하세요.

1 Joy has been in charge of keeping her girl happy.

2 Joy, Sadness, and all of the core memories get sucked out of Headquarters and end up lost deep inside Riley's mind.

3 Joy tells Sadness they need to get back to Headquarters to return the core memories.

4 Without her core memories in place, Riley's Islands of Personality begin to crumble away.

5 While traveling back to Headquarters, Joy and Sadness run into Riley's old imaginary friend, Bing Bong.

6 Riley has new friends, a new hockey team, and all five Emotions working together as a team.

A 알맞은 단어에 동그라미 하여 문장을 완성하세요.

1. Joy is an Emotion who lives in Riley's [head / mind] .

2. Everything is great until Riley and her family move to a new [city / country] .

3. Sadness touches a yellow memory and it turns [blue / white] !

4. Without Joy to run things, the other Emotions have to take [charge / care] .

5. Joy replays the memory and sees that Riley was really [mad / sad] .

6. Perhaps Sadness is [good / famous] for something after all.

7. Joy urges Sadness to take over the [console / bus] .

8. Riley yells for the bus driver to [go / stop] .

9. Riley cries and tells her [friends / parents] she misses Minnesota.

10. Before long, Riley adjusts to her new [life / job] in San Francisco.

B 다음 단어들을 이용해 우리말 뜻에 맞는 문장을 완성하세요.

1
| is | Joy | at her job | very good | . |

기쁨이는 그녀의 일을 매우 잘해요.

→ _____

2
| doesn't | Sadness | understand | Joy | . |

기쁨이는 슬픔이를 이해하지 못해요.

→ _____

3
| what to do | Riley's Emotions | don't know | . |

라일리의 감정들은 어떻게 해야 할지 몰라요.

→ _____

4
| alone | sits | she | and | sulks | . |

그녀는 혼자 앉아서 부루퉁해 있어요.

→ _____

5
| Riley | Anger | a terrible idea | gives | . |

버럭이는 라일리에게 끔찍한 생각을 주어요.

→ _____

6
| smiles | through | her tears | she | . |

그녀는 눈물을 흘리며 미소 지어요.

→ _____

STORY MAP

문장의 빈칸을 채워 이야기의 구조를 한눈에 정리해 보세요.

| parents | memories | loser | alone | feel | sad | terrible |

What Emotions Do

Joy tries to keep Sadness away from Riley's ① _____.

Fear, Anger, and Disgust make Riley act different.

Anger gives Riley a ⑤ _____ idea.

Joy urges Sadness to take over the console. Sadness touches the console.

What Happens

Riley's memories are happy ones.

Riley is a sore ② _____ at hockey tryouts.

She talks back to her ③ _____.

At school, she sits ④ _____ and sulks.

Riley is going to run away!

Riley begins to feel sad right away. Riley races home. She cries and tells her parents she misses Minnesota. Riley begins to ⑥ _____ better.

What Joy Understands

Joy understands that sometimes Riley needs to be ⑦ _____ before she can be happy again.

36

Disney

Tangled

Activities

A 다음 단어의 알맞은 우리말 뜻에 동그라미 하세요.

① remember (기억하다 / 잊어버리다) ② steal (치료하다 / 훔치다)

③ wonderful (궁금해하는 / 아주 멋진) ④ heartbroken (슬픔에 잠긴 / 사랑에 빠진)

⑤ thief (경찰 / 도둑) ⑥ person (사람 / 사물)

⑦ rescue (구조하다 / 고치다) ⑧ celebrate (유명하다 / 축하하다)

B 빈칸에 알맞은 단어를 써 넣어 퍼즐을 완성하세요.

Across	① 떠나다	② 깨닫다	③ 빛나다
Down	④ 달아나다	⑤ 마법의	⑥ 탑, 고층 건물

다음 단어를 사용하여 문장을 완성하세요.

wish	wither	determined	sparkling	return	holding

1 Once a year, on her birthday, Rapunzel saw _____ lights floating into the sky.

2 While trying to get away from Maximus, a _____ horse from the royal guard, Flynn found Rapunzel's hidden tower.

3 She asked him to let Flynn take her to see the sparkling lights. Maximus agreed. Rapunzel's _____ was about to come true!

4 Rapunzel saw a picture of the King and the Queen _____ their baby princess.

5 On shore, Flynn left Rapunzel and did not _____.

6 Without Rapunzel's magical hair, Mother Gothel _____ed away.

STORY Check

A 빈칸을 채워서 결과에 대한 단서를 완성하세요.

princess	realized	green	sparkling

Conclusion

Mother, I'm the lost ① _____.

[Clue 1]
Once a year, on her birthday, Rapunzel saw ② _____ lights floating into the sky. They seemed meant for her.

[Clue 2]
The Queen and the Princess had ③ _____ eyes — just like Rapunzel!

[Clue 3]
Rapunzel ④ _____ that she had been painting the kingdom's emblem, the golden sun, on her wall her entire life.

B 이야기의 순서에 맞게 알맞은 기호를 찾아 쓰세요.

ⓐ Rapunzel was swept up in a dance!
ⓑ One of the scary-looking men helped Flynn and Rapunzel escape.
ⓒ The people of the kingdom lit lanterns.
ⓓ Flynn and Rapunzel stopped in a pub.

C 다음 글에 알맞은 그림을 찾아 연결하세요.

1 Rapunzel had long, long hair and lived in a tall, tall tower.

2 Rapunzel showed Flynn a painting she had made of the lights and asked him to take her to see them.

3 Overjoyed, she saw the sparkling lights fill the sky.

4 Rapunzel remembered the picture of the lost princess and the Queen.

5 Without Rapunzel's magical hair, Mother Gothel withered away.

6 Rapunzel went to her real parents, the King and the Queen.

A 알맞은 단어에 동그라미 하여 문장을 완성하세요.

1 Rapunzel had long, long hair and lived in a tall, tall [tree / tower] .

2 She told Rapunzel that bad people wanted to take her [magical / short] hair.

3 Flynn had stolen the lost princess's [ring / crown] .

4 One of the scary-looking men helped Flynn and Rapunzel [escape / paint] .

5 The horse wanted to take Flynn to [home / jail] .

6 A little boy gave Rapunzel a small kingdom [flag / toy] .

7 At last, Rapunzel's wish came [out / true] .

8 She did not know that Flynn had been [tricked / sent] by evil Mother Gothel.

9 Mother Gothel was the only one who wanted to [steal / save] Rapunzel's magical hair.

10 Rapunzel was finally free of the [evil / kind] woman.

42

B 다음 단어들을 이용해 우리말 뜻에 맞는 문장을 완성하세요.

1

| never let | Mother Gothel | the tower | Rapunzel | leave | . |

고델은 라푼젤이 탑을 떠나는 것을 절대 허락하지 않았어요.

→ _____

2

| to hide | climbed up | Flynn | the tower | . |

플린은 숨기 위해 탑을 올라갔어요.

→ _____

3

| day | a | had | Flynn and Rapunzel | wonderful | . |

플린과 라푼젤은 환상적인 하루를 보냈어요.

→ _____

4

| and | left | Flynn | Rapunzel | did not return | . |

플린은 라푼젤을 두고 떠나 다시 돌아오지 않았어요.

→ _____

5

| tear | fell | single | golden | a | on Flynn's cheek | . |

금빛의 눈물 한 방울이 플린의 뺨에 떨어졌어요.

→ _____

6

| at last | had come | home | Rapunzel | ! |

라푼젤은 마침내 집으로 오게 되었어요!

→ _____

문장의 빈칸을 채워 이야기의 구조를 한눈에 정리해 보세요.

| eyes | cut | magical | hair | return | celebrating |

CAUSE

EFFECT

Rapunzel's hair was
①_____. It kept Mother
Gothel young and beautiful.

→

Mother Gothel stole Rapunzel
from her real parents, the
King and the Queen.

Mother Gothel told Rapunzel
that bad people wanted to
take her magical hair.

→

Rapunzel thought Flynn
wanted her ②_____.

The kingdom was ③_____
the birthday of the lost
princess.

→

A little boy gave Rapunzel
a small kingdom flag.

Fylnn had been tricked by evil
Mother Gothel. He had been
captured and put in jail.

→

On shore, Flynn left
Rapunzel and did not
④_____.

Flynn ⑤_____ Rapunzel's
hair.

→

Mother Gothel withered
away.

Rapunzel's golden tear
contained the last bit of
magic left inside.

→

Flynn's ⑥_____ opened.
He was all right!

Activities

WORD Check

A 다음 단어의 알맞은 우리말 뜻에 동그라미 하세요.

1 leader (지도자 / 마법사)

2 imagination (상상력 / 우정)

3 chase (뒤쫓다 / 구출하다)

4 toy (선물 / 장난감)

5 reunite (연습하다 / 다시 만나다)

6 accomplish (바꾸다 / 해내다)

7 antique (자장가 / 골동품)

8 free (자유로운 / 친절한)

B 빈칸에 알맞은 단어를 써 넣어 퍼즐을 완성하세요.

Across	① 완벽한	② 변하다, 바뀌다	③ 흔적
Down	④ 구출하다; 구출	⑤ ~에 닿다, 이르다	⑥ 살금살금 가다

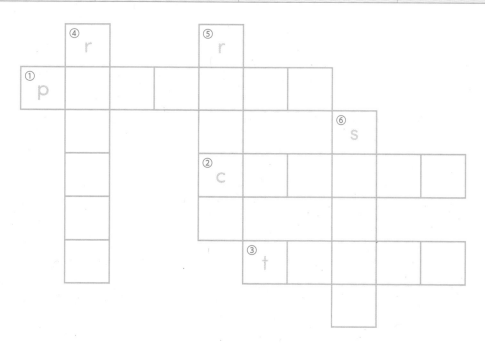

46

C 다음 단어를 사용하여 문장을 완성하세요.

exchange	life	capture
thrilled	orientation	soar

1. At kindergarten _____, she was a little nervous.

2. To Woody's surprise, Forky came to _____— just like the other toys!

3. She told her team to _____ Woody and Forky!

4. In _____ for Forky, he gave her his voice box.

5. Duke took a deep breath, revved his engine and _____ed over the crowd!

6. The toys found Bonnie. She was _____ to see Forky again!

A 이야기에 등장하는 장난감들에 대해 맞는 설명을 찾아 기호를 쓰세요.

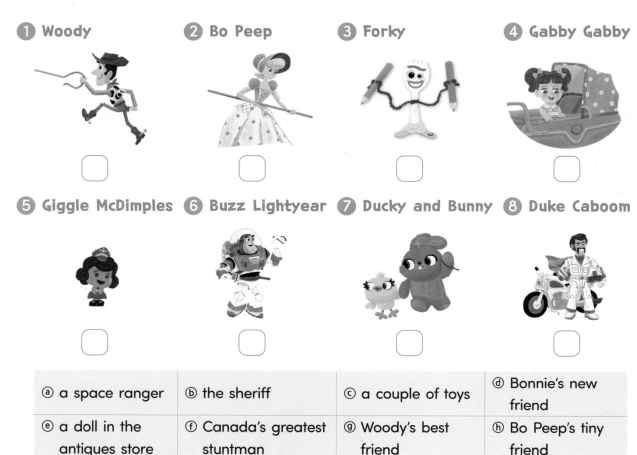

1 Woody

2 Bo Peep

3 Forky

4 Gabby Gabby

5 Giggle McDimples

6 Buzz Lightyear

7 Ducky and Bunny

8 Duke Caboom

| ⓐ a space ranger | ⓑ the sheriff | ⓒ a couple of toys | ⓓ Bonnie's new friend |
| ⓔ a doll in the antiques store | ⓕ Canada's greatest stuntman | ⓖ Woody's best friend | ⓗ Bo Peep's tiny friend |

B 이야기와 일치하는 문장에는 T, 일치하지 않는 문장에는 F에 동그라미 하세요.

1 Woody got a new kid. Her name was Bonnie.   T   F

2 Forky came to life—just like the other toys.   T   F

3 Gabby Gabby said she wanted Bo Peep's sheep.   T   F

4 Buzz Lightyear accidentally set Ducky and Bunny free.   T   F

C 다음 글에 알맞은 그림을 찾아 연결하세요.

1 Bo Peep was getting a new kid—and Woody was staying behind.

2 Years later, Woody got a new kid, too. Her name was Bonnie.

3 To Woody's surprise, Forky came to life—just like the other toys!

4 Buzz Lightyear met a couple of toys, Ducky and Bunny. Buzz accidently set both of them free!

5 Most of the group was too tired and scared to try a new plan. They decided to leave.

6 The toys found Bonnie. She was thrilled to see Forky again!

A 알맞은 단어에 동그라미 하여 문장을 완성하세요.

① Thankfully, his best friend, Bo Peep, was always there to lend a [hand / friend].

② Bonnie used her imagination to put them together to [draw / make] a new friend.

③ Sheriff Woody would never [believe / leave] anyone behind.

④ Gabby Gabby told her [doll / team] to capture Woody and Forky!

⑤ The [brave / old] space ranger followed their trail to a carnival.

⑥ The store's cat, Dragon, [cleaned / roamed] the aisles, looking for stray toys to gobble up.

⑦ In exchange for Forky, Woody gave her his [toy / voice] box.

⑧ Thanks to Duke, the toys zipped across the carnival on the [van / string].

⑨ The girl hugged the [ranger / doll] close just before she found her parents.

⑩ Woody realized that lost and lonely toys were everywhere, and he wanted to [help / sell] them.

B 다음 단어들을 이용해 우리말 뜻에 맞는 문장을 완성하세요.

1

| everything | one day, | then | changed | . |

그러던 어느 날, 모든 것이 바뀌었어요.

→ _____

2

| he was | a toy | at all | didn't think | he | . |

그는 자신이 장난감이라고 전혀 생각하지 않았어요.

→ _____

3

| out the window | he | jumped | after Forky | . |

그는 포키의 뒤를 따라 창문 밖으로 뛰어내렸어요.

→ _____

4

| to the next town | with Bonnie | Woody took | to catch up | Forky | . |

우디는 보니를 따라잡으려고 포키를 다음 도시로 데려갔어요.

→ _____

5

| set | accidentally | both of them | Buzz | free | ! |

버즈는 우연히 그들 둘을 자유롭게 풀어줬어요!

→ _____

6

| a | nearby | escaped | playground | to | Woody | . |

우디는 근처 놀이터로 도망쳤어요.

→ _____

STORY MAP

문장의 빈칸을 채워 이야기의 흐름을 한눈에 정리해 보세요.

break	friend	hugged	toys	cabinet	voice	escaped	capture

Woody got a new kid named Bonnie. Woody and Bonnie made a new ① _____, Forky.

When Bonnie's family went on a road trip, Forky made a ② _____ for it. Woody jumped out the window after Forky.

Woody and Forky went into the antiques store. Gabby Gabby told her team to ③ _____ Woody and Forky.

Woody ④ _____ to a nearby playground. There he saw Bo Peep and her friend, Giggle McDimples.

Woody and the toys went to the antiques store. Forky was trapped in a tall ⑤ _____.

Woody gave Gabby Gabby his ⑥ _____ box in exchange for Forky. And he would take her to Bonnie so she could have a kid, too.

At the carnival, a girl ⑦ _____ Gabby Gabby close. Gabby Gabby got a kid!

Woody wanted to help lost and lonely ⑧ _____. He knew that he could accomplish anything with his toy friends.

The Answers

BOOK QUIZ

Big Hero 6 Book Quiz   p.3

1. ②	2. ①	3. ④	4. ②	5. ①	6. ②
7. ④	8. ③	9. ④	10. ②	11. ③	12. ④
13. ①	14. ②	15. ①			

Ratatouille Book Quiz   p.5

1. ①	2. ②	3. ①	4. ③	5. ④	6. ③
7. ③	8. ①	9. ④	10. ③	11. ①	12. ①
13. ②	14. ③	15. ②			

Inside Out Book Quiz   p.7

1. ①	2. ②	3. ③	4. ②	5. ②	6. ①
7. ①	8. ②	9. ①	10. ③	11. ④	12. ②
13. ①	14. ①	15. ③			

Tangled Book Quiz   p.9

1. ①	2. ③	3. ③	4. ②	5. ②	6. ①
7. ①	8. ①	9. ④	10. ①	11. ④	12. ①
13. ③	14. ②	15. ①			

Toy Story 4 Book Quiz   p.11

1. ②	2. ③	3. ①	4. ④	5. ①	6. ③
7. ②	8. ①	9. ③	10. ②	11. ①	12. ①
13. ④	14. ①	15. ④			

BIG HERO 6 Activities

WORD Check p.14

A
① 발명품 ② 사고
③ 창조하다 ④ 탈출하다
⑤ 간호사 ⑥ 옷
⑦ 기계 ⑧ 구출하다

B

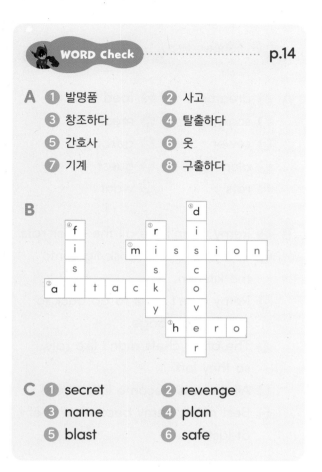

Crossword:
⑥d
④f ⑤r
i i
①m i s s i o n
s s c
②a t t a c k o
y v
③h e r o
r

C
① secret ② revenge
③ name ④ plan
⑤ blast ⑥ safe

SENTENCE Check p.18

A
① chip ② stolen
③ super ④ discovered
⑤ fist ⑥ lost
⑦ life ⑧ flew
⑨ nursing ⑩ Hero

B
① Hiro and Tadashi were brothers.
② Hiro invented tiny machines called microbots.
③ The team needed a plan to fight Yokai.
④ The suits gave everyone superpowers.
⑤ They would rescue Abigail.
⑥ Hiro and Abigail were safe.

STORY Check p.16

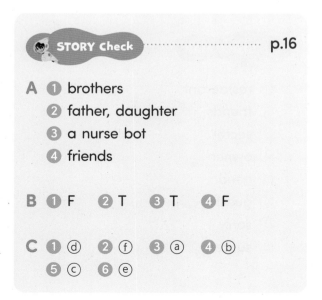

A
① brothers
② father, daughter
③ a nurse bot
④ friends

B ① F ② T ③ T ④ F

C ① ⓓ ② ⓕ ③ ⓐ ④ ⓑ
⑤ ⓒ ⑥ ⓔ

STORY MAP p.20

① mission
② revenge
③ attack
④ laboratory
⑤ space
⑥ safe

RATATOUILLE Activities

WORD Check
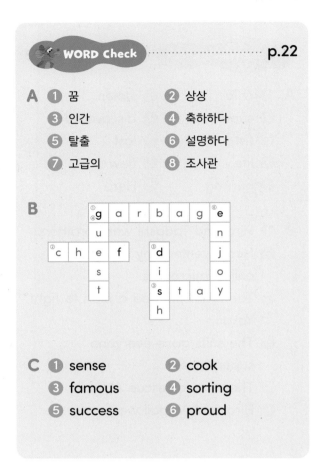

p.22

A
1. 꿈
2. 상상
3. 인간
4. 축하하다
5. 탈출
6. 설명하다
7. 고급의
8. 조사관

B

①⑥g	a	r	b	a	g	e	⑥e
u							n
②c	h	e	f	f		③d		j
s				i		o
t				④s	t	a	y
				h			

C
1. sense
2. cook
3. famous
4. sorting
5. success
6. proud

SENTENCE Check
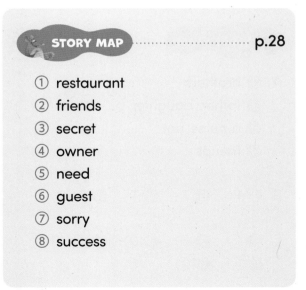

p.26

A
1. dreams
2. food
3. scary
4. meal
5. sewer
6. garbage
7. alone
8. guest
9. rats
10. want

B
1. Remy wasn't like all the other rats.
2. Remy fell from the skylight into the kitchen.
3. Remy didn't want to go back to smelling garbage.
4. The other chefs didn't like rats, so they left.
5. All the rats became little chefs!
6. Best of all, Remy became a chef at last.

STORY Check
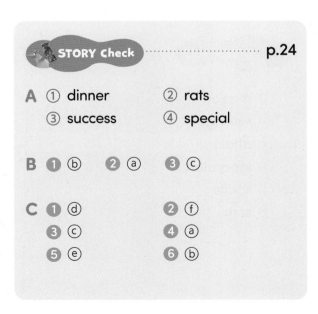

p.24

A
1. dinner
2. rats
3. success
4. special

B
1. ⓑ
2. ⓐ
3. ⓒ

C
1. ⓓ
2. ⓕ
3. ⓒ
4. ⓐ
5. ⓔ
6. ⓑ

STORY MAP

p.28

1. restaurant
2. friends
3. secret
4. owner
5. need
6. guest
7. sorry
8. success

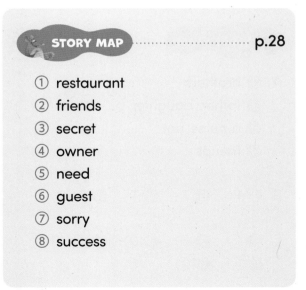

INSIDE OUT Activities

WORD Check p.30

A ① 일 ② 눈물
③ 상상의 ④ 안전한
⑤ 성격 ⑥ 긍정적인
⑦ 소리치다 ⑧ 기억

B

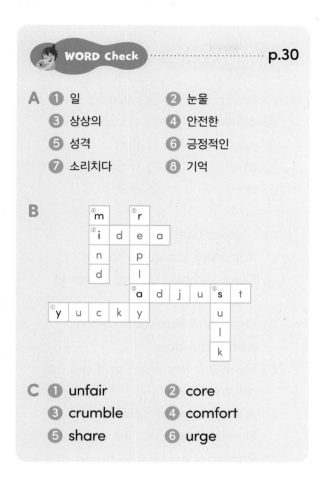

Crossword:
- ④ m, ⑤ r
- ② i d e a (with the 'e' connecting to r-column)
- n, p
- d, l
- ③ a d j u s t
- ① y u c k y ... u / l / k

C ① unfair ② core
③ crumble ④ comfort
⑤ share ⑥ urge

SENTENCE Check p.34

A ① mind ② city
③ blue ④ charge
⑤ sad ⑥ good
⑦ console ⑧ stop
⑨ parents ⑩ life

B ① Joy is very good at her job.
② Joy doesn't understand Sadness.
③ Riley's Emotions don't know what to do.
④ She sits alone and sulks.
⑤ Anger gives Riley a terrible idea.
⑥ She smiles through her tears.

STORY Check p.32

A ① Anger, ⓒ ② Sadness, ⓔ
③ Disgust, ⓑ ④ Joy, ⓓ
⑤ Fear, ⓐ

B ① T ② F ③ T ④ T

C ① ⓑ ② ⓓ
③ ⓐ ④ ⓕ
⑤ ⓔ ⑥ ⓒ

STORY MAP p.36

① memories
② loser
③ parents
④ alone
⑤ terrible
⑥ feel
⑦ sad

TANGLED Activities

WORD Check p.38

A ① 기억하다　② 훔치다
　③ 아주 멋진　④ 슬픔에 잠긴
　⑤ 도둑　⑥ 사람
　⑦ 구조하다　⑧ 축하하다

B
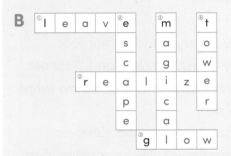

	l	e	a	v	e		m		t
					s		a		o
					c		g		w
		r	e	a	l	i	z	e	e
					p		c		r
					e		a		
							g	l	o	w

C ① sparkling　② determined
　③ wish　④ holding
　⑤ return　⑥ wither

STORY Check p.40

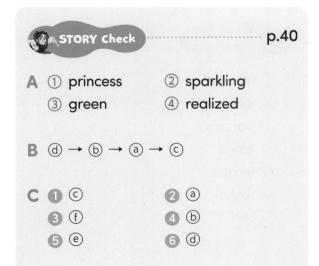

A ① princess　② sparkling
　③ green　④ realized

B ⓓ → ⓑ → ⓐ → ⓒ

C ① ⓒ　② ⓐ
　③ ⓕ　④ ⓑ
　⑤ ⓔ　⑥ ⓓ

SENTENCE Check p.42

A ① tower　② magical
　③ crown　④ escape
　⑤ jail　⑥ flag
　⑦ true　⑧ tricked
　⑨ steal　⑩ evil

B ① Mother Gothel never let
　Rapunzel leave the tower.
　② Flynn climbed up the tower to
　hide.
　③ Flynn and Rapunzel had a
　wonderful day.
　④ Flynn left Rapunzel and did not
　return.
　⑤ A single golden tear fell on
　Flynn's cheek.
　⑥ Rapunzel had come home at
　last!

STORY MAP p.44

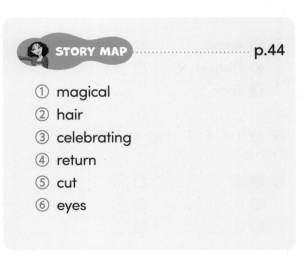

① magical
② hair
③ celebrating
④ return
⑤ cut
⑥ eyes

58

TOY STORY 4 Activities

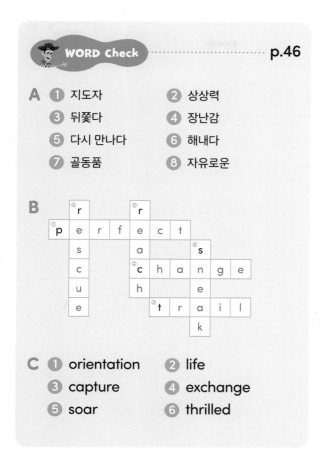

WORD Check ···· p.46

A ① 지도자 ② 상상력
③ 뒤쫓다 ④ 장난감
⑤ 다시 만나다 ⑥ 해내다
⑦ 골동품 ⑧ 자유로운

B

					r		r			
		p	e	r	f	e	c	t		
		s			a			s		
		c			c	h	a	n	g	e
		u			h			e		
		e			t	r	a	i	l	
					k					

C ① orientation ② life
③ capture ④ exchange
⑤ soar ⑥ thrilled

STORY Check ···· p.48

A ① ⓑ ② ⓖ
③ ⓓ ④ ⓔ
⑤ ⓗ ⑥ ⓐ
⑦ ⓒ ⑧ ⓕ

B ① T ② T ③ F ④ T

C ① ⓒ ② ⓕ ③ ⓐ
④ ⓑ ⑤ ⓓ ⑥ ⓔ

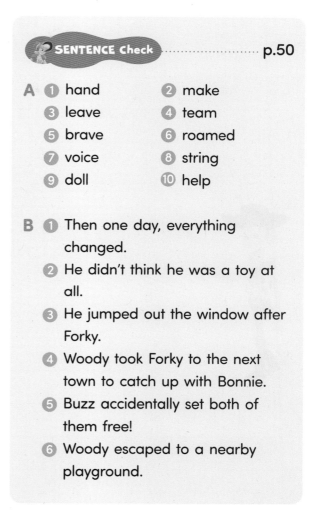

SENTENCE Check ···· p.50

A ① hand ② make
③ leave ④ team
⑤ brave ⑥ roamed
⑦ voice ⑧ string
⑨ doll ⑩ help

B ① Then one day, everything changed.
② He didn't think he was a toy at all.
③ He jumped out the window after Forky.
④ Woody took Forky to the next town to catch up with Bonnie.
⑤ Buzz accidentally set both of them free!
⑥ Woody escaped to a nearby playground.

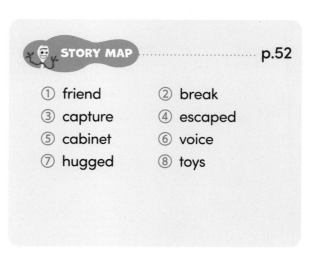

STORY MAP ···· p.52

① friend ② break
③ capture ④ escaped
⑤ cabinet ⑥ voice
⑦ hugged ⑧ toys

Disney · PIXAR
Story Collection 1

Activity Book

Part 1 북 퀴즈(Book Quiz)

읽은 내용을 얼마나 잘 이해했는지 북 퀴즈를 풀며 나의 리딩 실력을 점검합니다.
틀린 문제는 스토리북의 해당 내용을 다시 찾아 읽어보세요.

Part 2 학습 액티비티(Activities)

다양한 문제를 풀며 읽은 내용을 되돌아보고 어휘, 스토리 구조, 주요 문장 등을 다집니다.
문제 구성: Word Check • Story Check • Sentence Check • Story Map

Disney · PIXAR
Story Collection 1

Practice
Book

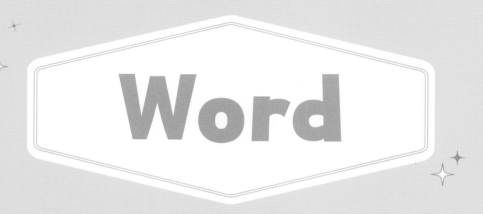

Word

Practice

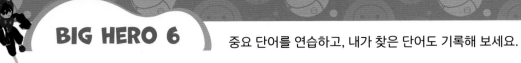

BIG HERO 6

중요 단어를 연습하고, 내가 찾은 단어도 기록해 보세요.

p.12-13

brother	몡 형제
create	몽 창조하다
fantastic	혱 환상적인
invention	몡 발명품
✏	

p.14-15

invent	몽 발명하다
allow	몽 가능하게 하다
tiny	혱 아주 작은
machine	몡 기계
large	혱 많은, 큰
object	몡 물건, 물체
impress	몽 감명을 주다
✏	

p.16-17

accident	몡 사고
left	leave(남기다)의 과거형, 과거분사
without	졘 ~없이

alone	부 혼자 형 외로운
p.18–19 discover	동 발견하다
villain	명 악당
stolen	steal(훔치다)의 과거분사
send	동 보내다
attack	동 공격하다
p.20–21 chase	동 뒤쫓다
barely	부 간신히, 가까스로
plan	명 계획 동 계획하다
fight	동 싸우다
p.22–23 suit	명 (특정한 활동에 입는) 옷
even	부 ~까지도, ~조차
wing	명 날개

fist	명 주먹	

p.24-25

dangerous	형 위험한	
pull	동 끌어당기다	
inside	전 ~의 안에	
lost	lose(잃다)의 과거형, 과거분사	
enter	동 들어가다	
risky	형 위험한	
revenge	명 복수	

p.26-27

sign	명 신호	
life	명 목숨, 생명	
portal	명 (다른 세계로 통하는) 관문	
rescue	동 구출하다 명 구출	

p.28-29

damage	동 피해를 입히다	

run out of	~을 다 써버리다	
hug	동 껴안다	
🖉		

p.30–31

use	동 사용하다	
last	명 마지막 남은 것	
blast	동 발사하다	
🖉		

p.32–33

safe	형 안전한	
gone	형 떠난, 가 버린	
even though	비록 ~일지라도	
still	부 아직, 여전히	
idea	명 발상, 생각	
🖉		

p.34

rebuilt	rebuild(다시 세우다)의 과거형, 과거분사	
ready	형 준비가 된	
action	명 행동, 조치	

RATATOUILLE

중요 단어를 연습하고, 내가 찾은 단어도 기록해 보세요.

p.40-41

rat　명 쥐

like　형 ~와 비슷한
　　　동 좋아하다

sense　명 감각

smell　명 후각
　　　동 냄새가 나다

taste　명 취향, 기호

dream　동 꿈꾸다　명 꿈

chef　명 요리사

p.42-43

job　명 직장

poison　명 독

food　명 음식, 먹이

sort　동 분류하다　명 종류

garbage　명 쓰레기

flee　동 달아나다

human　명 사람

float　동 떠가다

p.44–45

separate 　 통 분리하다, 떼어놓다

near 　 전 ~에서 가까이

French 　 형 프랑스의

restaurant 　 명 식당

p.46–47

idol 　 명 우상

pop up 　 불쑥 나타나다

imagination 　 명 상상

exciting 　 형 신나는, 흥미진진한

place 　 명 장소 통 두다, 놓다

scary 　 형 무서운

p.48–49

replace 　 통 교체하다

spill 　 통 엎지르다, 쏟다

secret 　 형 비밀의

meanwhile	튀 그 동안에	
rest	명 나머지	
colony	명 무리	
sewer	명 하수관	
find	동 찾다	
✎		

p.50—51

miss	동 그리워하다	
have to	~해야 한다	
hidden	hide(숨다)의 과거분사	
meal	명 식사	
celebrate	동 축하하다	
✎		

p.52—53

home	명 집	
of course	물론	
feel	동 (감정·기분을) 느끼다	
belong	동 소속감을 느끼다	

anymore	🔵 더 이상은
🖊	
p.54–55 explain	🟢 설명하다
often	🔵 자주
understand	🟢 이해하다
owner	🟡 주인
famous	🟣 유명한
attention	🟡 관심, 주목
🖊	
p.56–57 decide	🟢 결정하다
need	🟢 필요하다
argue	🟢 다투다
alone	🟣🔵 혼자, 외로운
🖊	
p.58–59 help	🟡 도움 🟢 돕다
special	🟣 특별한

guest	명 손님	
ask	통 요청하다	
dinner	명 저녁 식사	
success	명 성공 통 성공하다	
dish	명 요리; 접시	

p.60–61

chase away	~을 쫓아내다	
health inspector	명 위생 조사관	
close	통 닫다	
enjoy	통 즐기다	
fine	형 질 높은, 좋은	

p.62

best of all	무엇보다도, 특히	
at last	마침내	
proud	형 자랑스러운	

INSIDE OUT

중요 단어를 연습하고, 내가 찾은 단어도 기록해 보세요.

p.68-69

emotion	명 감정

mind	명 마음

ever since	그 이래 줄곧

in charge of	~을 담당해서

p.70-71

Headquarters	명 본부

express	동 표현하다

unfair	형 불공평한

yucky	형 역겨운

keep away	~에 가까이 가지 않다, 멀리 하다

console	명 콘솔, 제어장치

p.72-73

proud	형 자랑스러운

memory	명 기억

island	명 섬

personality	명 성격

honesty	몡 정직, 솔직함	
until	젠 ~할 때까지	
mess	몡 엉망인 상태	
🖉		

p.74–75

touch	통 만지다, 건드리다	
try	통 노력하다	
loose	혱 헐거워진, 느슨한	
suck out	통 빨려 나가다	
deep	뷔 깊이, 깊은 곳에	
🖉		

p.76–77

worried	혱 걱정하는	
positive	혱 긍정적인	
get back	돌아오다	
return	통 되돌려 놓다	
work	통 작동하다	
🖉		

12

share	통 공유하다, 나누다	
remember	통 기억하다	
awful	형 끔찍한	
replay	통 재생하다, 되풀이하다	
better	형 더 좋은	
🖊		

p.86-87

make it	해내다	
urge	통 ~하도록 설득하다	
take over	인수하다, 인계받다	
🖊		

p.88-90

right away	곧바로, 즉시	
yell	통 소리치다	
race	통 질주하다, 급히 가다	
miss	통 그리워하다	
tear	명 눈물	
adjust	통 적응하다	

TANGLED

중요 단어를 연습하고, 내가 찾은 단어도 기록해 보세요.

p.96-97

tower   명 탑

pull   동 ~을 잡아당기다

magical   형 마법의

stolen   steal(훔치다)의 과거분사

real   형 진짜의

herself   대 그녀 자신(스스로)

p.98-99

leave   동 떠나다

chameleon   명 카멜레온

year   명 해 (년/연)

light   명 등불 동 불을 켜다

wish   동 원하다 명 소원

meant   mean(의미하다)의 과거형, 과거분사

p.100-101

thief   명 도둑

hidden   형 숨겨진

climb	동 오르다	
besides	전 ~외에	
paint	동 (물감으로) 그리다	
agree	동 동의하다	
✎		

looking	형 ~으로 보이는	
friendly	형 친절한, 우호적인	
escape	동 탈출하다 명 탈출	
trap	동 가두다 명 덫	
cave	명 동굴	
glow	동 빛나다	
✎		

p.104–105

jail	명 감옥	
sparkle	동 반짝거리다	
come true	이루어지다	
wonderful	형 아주 멋진, 경이로운	

flag	몡 깃발
kingdom	몡 왕국
celebrate	통 기념하다
same	혱 똑같은
✏	

p.106—107

suddenly	뷔 갑자기
swept	sweep(휩쓸려가다)의 과거형, 과거분사
fun	혱 재미있는, 즐거운
so far	지금까지, 이 시점까지
✏	

p.108—109

people	몡 사람들
lantern	몡 손전등
fill	통 (가득) 채우다
world	몡 세계
outside	혱 외부의
✏	

p.110-111

return	통 돌아오다
heartbroken	형 가슴 아픈
trick	통 속이다
capture	통 포획하다
realize	통 알아차리다, 깨닫다
wall	명 담, 벽
life	명 삶

p.112-113

remember	통 기억하다
lost	형 잃어버린
know	통 알다
look alike	~같아 보이다
lie	통 거짓말하다

p.114-115

| arrive | 통 도착하다 |
| rescue | 통 구출하다 명 구출 |

hurt	통 다치게 하다	
badly	부 몹시, 심하게	
cut	통 자르다	
without	전 ~없이	
free	형 자유로운 통 풀어주다	
evil	형 사악한	
✏		

p.116–118

fall	통 떨어지다	
cheek	명 볼	
contain	통 ~을 포함하다	
magic	명 마법	
wait	통 기다리다	
daughter	명 딸	
at last	마침내	
belong	통 제자리에 있다, 소속감을 느끼다	
✏		

TOY STORY 4

중요 단어를 연습하고, 내가 찾은 단어도 기록해 보세요.

p.124–125

sheriff	몡 보안관
leader	몡 지도자, 대표
sometimes	몜 때때로, 가끔
help	몡 도움
lend a hand	도움을 주다

🖉

p.126–127

change	몸 변하다, 바뀌다
kid	몡 아이, 청소년
stay behind	뒤에 남다

🖉

p.128–129

kindergarten	몡 유치원
nervous	몧 불안한, 긴장되는
art supply	미술 용품
rustle up	재빨리 찾아주다
imagination	몡 상상력
put together	조립하다

p.130–131

surprise	통 놀라게 하다 / 명 놀라움
come to life	살아 움직이다
at all	조금도 (~ 아니다)
road trip	명 장거리 자동차 여행
leave behind	두고 가다

p.132–133

town	명 (소)도시, 시내
catch up with	~을 따라잡다
catch one's eye	~의 눈길을 붙잡다

p.134–135

instead	부 대신에
doll	명 인형
at first	처음에는
capture	통 붙잡다
escape	통 탈출하다 명 탈출
familiar	형 익숙한, 친숙한

travel	통 여행하다	
rescue	통 구출하다 명 구출	
✎		
p.136-137
search	통 찾다	
brave	형 용감한	
trail	명 흔적	
get stuck	갇히다	
couple	명 두 사람, 두 개	
accidentally	부 우연히, 뜻하지 않게	
free	통 풀어 주다	
✎		
p.138-139
sneak	통 살금살금 가다	
cabinet	명 캐비닛, 보관장	
roam	통 돌아다니다	
stray	형 길을 잃은, 주인이 없는	
figure out	생각해 내다	

as well as	~에 더하여, 게다가	
leap	통 뛰어오르다	
make it	성공하다, 해내다	
spot	통 발견하다	
chase	통 뒤쫓다	
hold on tight	꽉 잡다	
✏️		

p.140-141

try	통 시도하다	
leave	통 떠나다	
deal	명 거래	
exchange	명 교환	
reach	통 ~에 닿다, 이르다	
tie	통 묶다	
breath	명 (한 번 들이쉬는) 숨	
engine	명 엔진	
✏️		

p.142–143	
soar	동 날아오르다
crowd	명 사람들, 군중
p.144–145	
thanks to	~덕분에
zip	동 쌩 하고 가다
string	명 끈
notice	동 알아차리다
close	부 가까이, 바싹
thrilled	형 신이 난
reunite	동 재회하다
p.146	
realize	동 깨닫다
lost	형 길을 잃은
lonely	형 외로운
accomplish	동 해내다, 성취하다

Sentence

Practice

BIG HERO 6

빈칸에 알맞은 단어를 채워 문장을 완성하세요.

1 히로와 타다시는 형제였어요.

Hiro and Tadashi were [   ]s.

2 그들은 환상적인 새로운 발명품을 만들어내는 것을 굉장히 좋아했어요!

They loved to create fantastic new [   ]s!

3 타다시는 베이맥스라고 하는 간호 로봇을 발명했어요. "안녕하세요. 베이맥스예요."

Tadashi [   ]ed a nurse bot named Baymax. "Hello. I am Baymax."

4 베이맥스의 안에는 특별한 간호 칩이 들어있어서, 베이맥스가 아픈 사람들을 도울 수 있었어요.

A special nursing chip inside Baymax [   ]ed him to help sick people.

5 히로는 마이크로봇이라고 하는 아주 작은 기계들을 발명했어요.

Hiro invented [   ] machines called microbots.

6 그 작은 마이크로봇들은 함께 일하면서 훨씬 더 큰 물체를 만들어낼 수 있었어요!

Working together, the little microbots could create much larger [   ]s!

7 로봇 공학 선생님인 캘러한 교수는 깊은 인상을 받았어요.

Professor Callaghan, a robotics teacher, was [   ]ed.

8 학교에서 사고가 일어난 후, 히로는 형 없이 혼자 남게 되었어요.

After an [   ] at school, Hiro was left without his brother.

9 그는 혼자인 듯한 외로움을 느꼈어요. 하지만 히로는 혼자가 아니었어요.

He felt all alone. But Hiro was not [   ].

Word Box

brother 명 형제	**object** 명 물체	**alone** 형 부 혼자, 외로운	**allow** 동 가능하게 하다	**tiny** 형 아주 작은
invention 명 발명품	**impress** 동 깊은 인상을 주다	**accident** 명 사고	**invent** 동 발명하다	

⑩ 그에겐 타다시의 간호 로봇인 베이맥스가 있었어요! 히로와 베이맥스는 요카이라고 하는 악당이 마이크로봇들을 훔쳐간 것을 알게 됐어요!

He had Tadashi's nurse bot, Baymax! Hiro and Baymax discovered that a [＿＿＿＿] named Yokai had stolen the microbots!

⑪ 요카이는 마이크로봇 한 무리를 보내 그들을 공격하게 했어요.

Yokai sent a swarm of microbots to [＿＿＿＿] them.

⑫ 히로의 친구들은 돕고 싶어 했어요. 하지만 요카이가 그들을 쫓아왔어요!

Hiro's friends wanted to help but Yokai [＿＿＿＿]d them!

⑬ 히로와 그의 친구들은 간신히 도망쳐 목숨만 겨우 건졌어요!

Hiro and his friends [＿＿＿＿] escaped with their lives!

⑭ 히로의 팀은 요카이와 싸울 계획이 필요했어요.

The team needed a plan to [＿＿＿＿] Yokai.

⑮ 히로는 그들 각각을 위해 첨단 기술의 굉장한 의상을 발명했어요!

Hiro invented [＿＿＿＿] super suits for each of them!

⑯ 그 의상은 모두에게 초능력을 주었어요!

The suits gave everyone [＿＿＿＿]s!

⑰ 베이맥스까지도 날개와 로켓 주먹이 달린 새로운 의상을 받았어요!

Even Baymax got a new suit——with wings and a rocket [＿＿＿＿]!

⑱ 요카이가 비밀 실험실을 공격하자, 위험한 문이 열렸어요.

When Yokai attacked a secret laboratory, a dangerous [＿＿＿＿] opened up.

Word Box

fight	superpower	chase	barely	villain
통 싸우다	명 막강한 힘, 초능력	통 쫓아가다	부 간신히	명 악당
high-tech	attack	portal	fist	
형 첨단 기술의	통 공격하다	명 정문, 포털	명 주먹	

19 그것은 모든 것을 안으로 끌어당기기 시작했어요! 그리고 히로는 요카이가 캘러한 교수라는 것을 알아차렸어요!

It started to [   ] everything inside! Then Hiro discovered that Yokai was Professor Callaghan!

20 캘러한의 딸인 아비게일은 위험한 임무를 맡아 그 문으로 들어갔다가 실종되었어요.

Callaghan's daughter, Abigail, had been lost when she entered the portal on a [   ] mission.

21 그는 그 책임이 있는 과학자에게 복수를 하고 싶었던 거예요.

He wanted [   ] on the scientist who was responsible.

22 베이맥스의 감지기는 생명체의 신호를 발견했어요.

Baymax's sensors were picking up signs of [   ].

23 히로와 베이맥스는 용감하게 그 문 안으로 날아 들어갔어요.

Hiro and Baymax bravely [   ] into the portal.

24 그들은 아비게일을 구출하려 했어요!

They would [   ] Abigail!

25 히로와 베이맥스는 없어졌던 아비게일의 우주선을 찾아냈어요!

Hiro and Baymax [   ] Abigail's lost space pod.

26 그러나 베이맥스는 손상을 입어서 동력이 빠르게 떨어져가고 있었어요!

But Baymax was [   ]d and running out of power fast!

27 베이맥스에게는 그들을 집으로 보낼 계획이 있었어요. 히로는 그의 친구를 껴안고 작별 인사를 했어요.

Baymax had a plan to get them home. Hiro [   ]ged his friend good-bye.

28 베이맥스는 그의 주먹에 히로와 아비게일을 싣고 그것을 문 밖으로 발사하는 데 마지막 남은 힘을 썼어요.

Then Baymax used the last of his power to [   ] his fist out of the portal, taking Hiro and Abigail with it.

Word Box

risky	life	revenge	pull	flew
형 위험한	명 생명	명 복수	통 당기다	fly(날다)의 과거형
hug	found	blast	rescue	damage
통 껴안다	find(찾다)의 과거형	통 발사하다	통 구출하다	통 손상을 입히다

29 히로와 아비게일은 안전했어요!

Hiro and Abigail were [　　　　　]!

30 하지만 베이맥스는 없었어요.

But Baymax was [　　　　　].

31 히로는 베이맥스를 잃긴 했지만, 그에게는 아직 로봇의 간호 칩이 있었어요.

[　　　　　] [　　　　　] Hiro had lost Baymax, he still had the robot's nursing chip.

32 그것은 히로에게 아이디어를 주었어요! 히로는 베이맥스를 다시 만들었어요!

That gave him an idea! Hiro [　　　　　] Baymax!

33 빅 히어로 6인조는 다시 돌아왔고, 작전 준비가 완료되었어요!

BIG HERO 6 was back and ready for [　　　　　]!

Word Box

safe	even though	action	rebuilt	gone
형 안전한	~이긴 하지만	명 작전, 활동	rebuild(다시 조립하다)의 과거형	형 떠난, 가 버린

RATATOUILLE 빈칸에 알맞은 단어를 채워 문장을 완성하세요.

1 이것은 큰 꿈을 가진 작은 쥐 레미에 관한 이야기예요.

This is the story of Remy, a little [   ] with big dreams.

2 레미는 다른 모든 쥐들과는 달랐어요.

Remy wasn't like all the [   ] rats.

3 한가지 예로, 그는 후각이 엄청나게 발달했어요.

For one thing, he had an [   ] sense of SMELL.

4 또 그는 고급 음식을 좋아하는 취향이 있었어요.

He also had a [   ] for finer food.

5 바로 그렇기 때문에 레미는 셰프가 되는 것을 꿈꿨어요.

And THAT is why Remy [   ]ed of being a CHEF!

6 하지만 레미의 아빠인 쟝고는 레미가 다른 직업을 가지도록 했어요. 쥐약이 있는지 확인하는 일이었죠.

But Django, Remy's father, had another job for him... [   ] checker.

7 퇴비 더미는 쥐들이 먹이를 찾는 곳이었어요.

The compost heap was where the rats got all their [   ].

8 레미는 안전한 쓰레기와 나쁜 쓰레기를 분류하는 중요한 직업을 가졌어요.

Remy had the important job of [   ]ing the safe garbage from the bad garbage.

9 이것은 그의 꿈에 포함되는 일이 아니었어요.

This was NOT [   ] of his dream.

10 어느 날, 쥐들은 집을 떠나 도망쳐야 했어요.

One day, the rats had to [   ] their home.

Word Box

dream 통 꿈꾸다	other 형 다른	food 명 음식, 먹이	poison 명 독, 독약	taste 명 취향, 기호
part 명 일부	sort 통 분류하다	extraordinary 형 비범한	rat 명 쥐	flee 통 도망치다

11. 어떤 사람이 그들을 발견한 거예요!

A HUMAN had [ ]ed them!

12. 그 사람이 그들을 쫓아오자, 쥐들은 탈출선으로 달려가서 하수관으로 떠내려갔어요.

As the human [ ]d them, the rats ran to their ESCAPE boats and floated into the sewers.

13. 레미는 다른 쥐들과 떨어져서 파리에 있는 고급 프랑스 레스토랑 근처로 가게 되었어요.

Remy got [ ]d from the others and ended up near a fancy French restaurant——in PARIS.

14. 한때 그 레스토랑의 주인은 레미의 우상인, 지금은 세상을 떠난 위대한 셰프 오귀스트 구스토였어요.

The restaurant used to belong to Remy's [ ], the late and great chef, Auguste Gusteau.

15. 구스토가 레미의 상상 속에서 불쑥 나타났어요.

Now Gusteau [ ]ped up in Remy's IMAGINATION.

16. 그리곤 아이쿠! 레미는 채광창에서 주방으로 떨어졌어요.

Then——whoops! Remy fell from the [ ] into the kitchen.

17. 그 레스토랑은 레미에게 신나는 장소였지만, 무서운 곳이기도 했어요.

The restaurant was an [ ] place for Remy, but it was SCARY, too.

18. 주방에서 레미는 청소부 소년이 쏟은 수프를 대신하기 위해 수프 한 냄비를 요리했어요.

In the kitchen, Remy cooked a pot of soup to replace what the garbage boy had [ ]ed.

19. 그 청소부 소년의 이름은 링귀니였어요.

The garbage boy was [ ]d Linguini.

Word Box

spill 통 쏟다, 흘리다	chase 통 뒤쫓다	separate 통 떨어지다, 분리하다	pop up 불쑥 나타나다	name 통 이름을 짓다
skylight 명 천장에 낸 채광창	exciting 형 신나는	discover 통 발견하다	idol 명 우상	

Ratatouille 31

20 그 일 후, 링귀니와 레미는 친구가 되었어요.

After that, Linguini and Remy [   ] friends.

21 그리고 그들은 비밀 요리 팀이 되었죠. 쉿!

AND they were a [   ] cooking team. SHHHH!

22 한편, 쟝고와 나머지 쥐 무리는 파리 지하의 캄캄하고 축축한 하수관에 새로운 집을 만들었어요.

Meanwhile, Django and the rest of the rat [   ] made a new home in the dark, wet sewers under Paris.

23 레미가 없으니 상황이 예전과 같지 않았어요.

[   ] weren't the same without Remy.

24 쟝고는 언젠가 아들을 찾기를 바라고 있었어요.

Django kept hoping he would find his [   ] one day.

25 하지만 레미는 행복했어요.

But Remy was [   ].

26 그는 가족이 그리웠지만, 이 세상에서 자신이 있을 곳을 찾아냈어요.

He did [   ] his family, but he had found his place in the world.

27 링귀니와 레미는 같이 일하면서 훌륭한 음식을 만들었어요. 레미는 계속 숨어 지내야 했지만요.

Working together, Linguini and Remy made great food, [   ] [   ] Remy had to stay hidden.

28 셰프들은 주방에 쥐가 있는 걸 원하지 않았거든요!

The human chefs did not [   ] a rat in their kitchen!

29 어느 날 셰프들은 멋진 음식을 요리한 후 주방에서 신나게 먹고 마셨어요.

Once, after cooking a wonderful meal, the chefs [   ]d in the kitchen.

Word Box

things	secret	even though	miss	son
몡 상황	혱 비밀의	~이긴 하지만	동 그리워하다	몡 아들
celebrate	colony	became	want	happy
동 축하하다, 축배를 들다	몡 집단	become(~이 되다)의 과거형	동 원하다	혱 행복한

32

30 레미도 뒷골목에서 마음껏 마셨는데, 그곳에서 형인 에밀을 발견했어요!

Remy celebrated, too, in the back [＿＿＿＿], where he found his brother EMILE!

31 에밀은 레미를 하수관에 있는 새로운 쥐 마을에 있는 집으로 데려갔어요.

Emile took Remy [＿＿＿＿] to the rats' new colony in the sewer.

32 물론, 쟝고는 레미를 다시 만나 행복했어요!

[＿＿] [＿＿＿＿], Django was HAPPY to see Remy again!

33 하지만 레미는 자신이 더는 쥐들과 같이 있을 존재가 아닌 것처럼 느껴졌어요.

But Remy didn't feel for now he belonged with the rats [＿＿＿＿].

34 그는 냄새나는 쓰레기로 다시 돌아가고 싶지 않았어요.

He didn't want to go back to [＿＿＿＿] garbage.

35 "저에게는 친구들도 있고, 살 곳도 있고, 사랑하는 일도 있어요." 레미는 아빠에게 설명하려 했어요.

"I have friends, a place to live, work that I love," Remy tried to [＿＿＿＿] to his dad.

36 "자주 올게요." 그가 말했어요.

"I'll come back [＿＿＿＿]," he said.

37 하지만 우선 그의 새 집과 레스토랑으로 돌아가야 했어요.

But for now he had to [＿＿＿＿] to his new home and the restaurant.

38 레미의 아빠는 이해할 수 없었어요. 레미는 작은 셰프로 다시 돌아왔어요.

Remy's dad didn't [＿＿＿＿]. Remy went back to being a little chef.

39 한편 링귀니는 사랑에 빠졌어요!

Meanwhile, Linguini was [＿＿＿＿]ing in love!

Word Box

of course 물론	alley 명 골목	return 통 돌아오다	smelling 형 냄새나는	fall in love 사랑에 빠지다
understand 통 이해하다	often 부 자주	home 명 집	explain 통 설명하다	anymore 부 더 이상

40 곧 링귀니는 자신이 레스토랑의 주인이라는 것을 알게 되었어요!

Soon Linguini found out that he was the [   ] of the restaurant!

41 그리고 레스토랑은 아주 유명해지고 있었어요.

And the restaurant was becoming very [   ].

42 링귀니는 관심을 받아서 좋았어요. 링귀니는 이제 더 이상 레미가 필요 없다고 결정했어요.

Linguini enjoyed the [   ]. Linguini decided he didn't need Remy anymore.

43 그들은 말다툼을 했어요. 레미는 몹시 슬펐고, 혼자라는 느낌이 들었어요. 이제 그의 가족은 누구일까요?

They ARGUED. Remy felt very SAD and [   ]. Who was his family now?

44 하지만 링귀니는 도움이 필요했어요. 그는 특별한 손님을 위해 특별한 저녁 식사를 요리해야 했거든요.

But Linguini needed HELP. He had to cook a special dinner for a special [   ].

45 그래서 링귀니는 레미에게 미안하다고 했어요.

And Linguini told Remy he was [   ].

46 다른 셰프들은 쥐를 좋아하지 않았기 때문에 떠나버렸어요.

The other chefs didn't like rats, so they [   ].

47 쟝고는 링귀니가 레미에게 친절하게 대하는 것을 보았어요.

Django saw Linguini being [   ] to Remy.

48 그는 쥐 무리에 있는 모두에게 특별한 저녁 요리를 만드는 것에 협력하라고 부탁했어요.

He asked everyone in the rat colony to [   ] in to help make the special dinner.

49 모든 쥐들이 작은 셰프가 되었어요! 쥐들의 도움으로 음식은 성공적으로 잘 만들어졌어요.

All the rats became little chefs! With the rats' help, the meal was a [   ].

Word Box

owner	famous	kind	left	guest
명 주인	형 유명한	형 친절한	leave(떠나다)의 과거형	명 손님
sorry	**alone**	**success**	**pitch in**	**attention**
형 미안한	형 혼자인, 외로운	명 성공	협력하다	명 관심

34

(50) 그 특별한 요리는 라따뚜이였어요!

The SPECIAL dish was [   ]!

(51) 쥐들은 레미를 도와 쥐가 있다는 이유로 레스토랑 영업을 중지시킨 위생 검사관을 쫓아버렸어요.

The rats also helped Remy CHASE away the health [   ] who still CLOSED the restaurant for having rats.

(52) 그 일로 레미와 친구들에게 아이디어가 떠올랐어요.

That gave Remy and his friends an [   ].

(53) 그들은 새 레스토랑을 열었어요!

They [   ]ed a NEW one!

(54) 레미의 무리는 그 레스토랑에서 식사를 했어요. 그들이 원해왔던 온갖 종류의 좋은 음식을 즐겼어요.

And Remy's colony [   ] at the restaurant, too——enjoying all the fine food they could ever want.

(55) 무엇보다도, 레미는 마침내 셰프가 됐어요.

Best of all, Remy became a chef [   ] [   ].

(56) "네가 무엇이든 정말 자랑스럽구나." 쟝고가 말했어요.

"I am [   ] of you no matter what," Django said.

Word Box

ratatouille 명 라따뚜이(양파, 가지, 호박, 토마토로 만든 스튜)	**inspector** 명 검사관, 조사관	**proud** 형 자랑스러운
at last 마침내	**ate** eat(먹다)의 과거형	**open** 통 개업하다
		idea 명 아이디어

빈칸에 알맞은 단어를 채워 문장을 완성하세요.

1 이쪽은 기쁨이에요.

This is ⬚.

2 그녀는 라일리의 마음 속에 사는 감정이에요.

She is an ⬚ who lives in Riley's mind.

3 라일리가 태어난 이후로 줄곧, 기쁨이는 라일리의 행복을 책임져 왔어요. 기쁨이는 이 일을 아주 잘한답니다!

Ever since Riley was born, Joy has been in ⬚ of keeping her girl happy. Joy is very good at her job!

4 기쁨이는 라일리의 마음 속 본부에서 라일리의 다른 감정들과 함께 일해요.

Joy works in ⬚ inside Riley's mind, along with Riley's other Emotions.

5 소심이는 라일리가 안전하도록 도와요.

⬚ helps keep Riley safe.

6 버럭이는 라일리가 어떤 일이 부당하다는 생각이 들 때 자신의 의사를 표현하도록 도와요. 브로콜리를 먹어야 하는 것과 같은 일이 있을 때요.

⬚ helps Riley express herself if she thinks something is unfair——like having to eat broccoli.

7 까칠이는 라일리가 브로콜리 같은 구역질나는 것들을 멀리하도록 도와줘요.

⬚ helps Riley stay away from yucky things——like broccoli.

8 그리고 또 슬픔이가 있어요. 기쁨이는 슬픔이를 이해하지 못해요.

And then there is ⬚. Joy doesn't understand Sadness.

9 그녀는 슬픔이를 감정 제어 장치에서, 그리고 라일리의 기억에서 멀리 떼어 놓으려고 노력해요.

She tries to keep Sadness away from the ⬚——and from Riley's memories.

Word Box

charge	emotion	anger	Headquarters	joy
몡 책임	몡 감정	몡 화, 분노	몡 본부	몡 기쁨
fear	disgust	console	sadness	
몡 두려움	몡 혐오감	몡 콘솔, 제어장치	몡 슬픔	

⑩ 기쁨이는 라일리의 기억 대부분이 행복한 것들이라 자랑스럽고, 기억들을 계속 그런 식으로 유지하기를 원해요!

Joy is [   ] that most of Riley's memories are happy ones, and she wants to keep them that way!

⑪ 가장 중요한 기억들은 핵심 기억들이라고 불려요.

The most important memories are called [   ] memories.

⑫ 그것들은 성격의 섬들에 에너지를 공급해요. 가족 섬, 정직 섬, 하키 섬, 우정 섬, 그리고 엉뚱 섬 같은 것들이요. 그리고 라일리를 라일리답게 만들지요.

They [   ] the Islands of Personality——Family Island, Honesty Island, Hockey Island, Friendship Island, and Goofball Island——and make Riley, Riley.

⑬ 라일리네 가족이 새로운 도시로 이사가기 전까지는 모든 것이 훌륭해요.

Everything is great until Riley and her family [   ] to a new city.

⑭ 라일리는 친구들이 보고 싶고, 새 집은 엉망진창이고, 피자에는 브로콜리가 들어 있어요! 라일리의 감정들은 무얼 해야 할지 모르겠어요.

Riley misses her friends, their new house is a [   ], and the pizza has broccoli on it! Riley's Emotions don't know what to do.

⑮ 슬픔이가 노란 기억을 건드리자 그것이 파란 색으로 변해요!

Sadness touches a yellow memory and it [   ]s blue!

⑯ 기쁨이가 슬픔이를 막으려 하지만, 라일리의 핵심 기억은 충격을 받아 느슨하게 풀려버려요.

When Joy tries to stop her, all of Riley's core memories get knocked [   ].

⑰ 기쁨이와 슬픔이, 그리고 모든 핵심 기억들은 본부 밖으로 빨려 나가요. 그리고 결국은 라일리의 마음 깊은 곳에서 길을 잃고 말아요.

Joy, Sadness, and all of the core memories get [   ]ed out of Headquarters and end up lost deep inside Riley's mind.

Word Box

proud 형 자랑스러워하는	**core** 형 핵심적인	**suck out** 빨려 나가다	**turn** 동 바뀌다
mess 명 엉망인 상태	**move** 동 이사하다	**loose** 형 헐거워진, 느슨한	**power** 동 동력을 공급하다

18 기쁨이는 걱정스러워요. 자신이 라일리를 행복하게 만들어 주지 않으면 그녀에게 무슨 일이 일어날까요?

Joy is worried. What will [   ] to Riley if she's not there to make her happy?

19 기쁨이는 계속 긍정적으로 생각하려고 노력해요.

Joy tries to stay [   ].

20 그녀는 슬픔이에게 본부로 돌아가서 핵심 기억을 되돌려 놓아야 한다고 말해요.

She tells Sadness they need to get back to Headquarters to [   ] the core memories.

21 그것이 성격 섬을 다시 작동하게 할 유일한 방법이에요.

That's the only way the Islands of [   ] will work again.

22 본부에서는 상황이 제대로 돌아가고 있지 않아요. 상황을 관리하던 기쁨이가 없으니, 다른 감정들이 책임을 맡아야만 해요.

Things aren't going well back at Headquarters. Without Joy to [   ] things, the other Emotions have to take charge.

23 소심이, 버럭이, 그리고 까칠이는 라일리가 다르게 행동하도록 만들어요.

Fear, Anger, and Disgust make Riley [   ] different.

24 라일리는 하키 입단 테스트에서 떨어진 것을 깨끗이 인정하지 못하고 불평해요.

She's a sore [   ] at hockey tryouts.

25 그녀는 부모님에게 말대꾸를 해요. 학교에서는 혼자 앉아 골을 내요.

She talks back to her parents. At school, she sits alone and [   ]s.

26 핵심 기억이 제자리에 없기 때문에, 라일리의 성격 섬들은 무너지기 시작해요!

Without her core memories in place, Riley's Islands of Personality begin to [   ] away!

Word Box

act 통 행동하다	**positive** 형 긍정적인	**sulk** 통 부루퉁하다, 못마땅해 하다	**personality** 명 성격	**run** 통 관리하다, 운영하다
happen 통 (일이) 일어나다	**loser** 명 (경쟁에서) 패자	**crumble** 통 무너지다	**return** 통 되돌려 놓다	

38

㉗ 본부로 다시 돌아가는 동안, 기쁨이와 슬픔이는 라일리의 오래된 상상 속 친구 빙봉과 우연히 마주쳐요.

While traveling back to Headquarters, Joy and Sadness run into Riley's old [   ] friend, Bing Bong.

㉘ 그는 라일리가 자신을 잊어버린 것에 슬퍼해요. 기쁨이는 슬픔이가 빙봉을 위로하는 것을 보고 놀라요.

He is sad because Riley has forgotten him. Joy is surprised to see that Sadness is able to [   ] Bing Bong.

㉙ 아마 어떤 것을 위해서는 슬픔이가 있어야 좋을 때도 있나 봐요.

[   ] Sadness is good for something after all.

㉚ 그러는 동안, 버럭이는 라일리가 끔찍한 생각을 떠올리도록 해요. 그녀는 가출할 거예요!

Meanwhile, Anger gives Riley a terrible idea. She is going to run [   ]!

㉛ 본부로 가는 여정에서, 기쁨이는 자신과 슬픔이가 가장 좋아하는 기억을 공유하고 있다는 것에 놀라요.

On their journey, Joy is surprised to find out that she and Sadness [   ] the same favorite memory.

㉜ 전에 미네소타에서 하키 게임을 한 다음의 일이었어요. 슬픔이는 라일리가 결승 샷을 놓쳐서 기분이 나빴던 것을 기억해요.

It was after a hockey game back in Minnesota. Sadness remembers that Riley [   ]ed the winning shot and felt awful.

㉝ 기쁨이는 기억을 다시 떠올려 보고는 라일리가 정말 슬펐다는 것을 알게 돼요.

Joy [   ]s the memory and sees that Riley was really sad.

㉞ 하지만 그때 가족들과 친구들이 그녀의 기분이 나아지도록 해주었어요.

But then her family and friends made her feel [   ].

㉟ 기쁨이는 이제 이해해요. 라일리도 때로는 슬퍼야 그 후에 다시 행복해질 수 있다는 것을요.

Joy now understands that sometimes Riley [   ]s to be sad before she can be happy again.

Word Box

comfort	run away	perhaps	imaginary	share
图 위로하다	가출하다	图 아마	图 상상의	图 공유하다
miss	replay	need	better	
图 놓치다	图 다시 (떠올려) 보다	图 ~할 필요가 있다	图 good(좋은)의 비교급	

36 기쁨이와 슬픔이는 마침내 본부로 돌아와요. 그리고 그들은 마침 딱 제때 도착했어요. 라일리가 버스를 타고 있거든요!

Joy and Sadness [_____] make it back to Headquarters. And they're just in time— Riley is on a bus!

37 기쁨이는 슬픔이에게 감정 제어 장치를 맡으라고 강력하게 권해요.

Joy [_____]s Sadness to take over the console.

38 모든 감정들이 슬픔이가 감정 제어 장치를 만지는 것을 지켜봐요. 라일리는 곧바로 슬픔을 느끼기 시작해요.

All the Emotions watch as Sadness touches the console. Riley begins to feel sad [_____] [_____].

39 그녀는 부모님이 보고 싶어요. 버스 기사님에게 세워 달라고 소리쳐요.

She misses her parents. She [_____]s for the bus driver to stop.

40 라일리는 집으로 달려가요. 그녀는 부모님에게 미네소타가 그립다고 울면서 말해요.

Riley [_____]s home. She cries and tells her parents she misses Minnesota.

41 부모님도 미네소타가 그립다고 말해요. 라일리는 기분이 나아지기 시작해요. 그녀는 울면서 웃어요.

Her parents say they miss Minnesota, too. Riley begins to feel better. She smiles through her [_____]s.

42 얼마 후, 라일리는 샌프란시스코의 새로운 생활에 적응해요.

Before long, Riley [_____]s to her new life in San Francisco.

43 그녀에겐 새 친구들이 있고, 새 하키팀이 있고, 한 팀으로 함께 일하는 다섯 감정들이 있어요.

She has new friends, a new hockey team, and all five Emotions working together [_____] a team.

Word Box

finally	adjust	right away	yell
부 마침내	동 적응하다	곧바로	동 소리치다
urge	tear	as	race
동 강력히 권고하다	명 눈물	전 ~로서	동 급히 가다

40

TANGLED

빈칸에 알맞은 단어를 채워 문장을 완성하세요.

1 라푼젤은 머리카락이 아주 길었고, 높고 높은 탑에 살았어요.

Rapunzel had long, long hair and lived in a tall, tall ⬚.

2 그녀의 머리카락은 그 탑의 높이만큼이나 길었어요.

Her hair was ⬚ long ⬚ the tower was tall.

3 어머니 고델은 매일 집에 오면 이렇게 외쳤어요. "라푼젤, 네 머리카락을 내려라!"

When Mother Gothel came home every day, she called, "Rapunzel, ⬚ down your hair!"

4 그리고 라푼젤은 어머니 고델을 탑 안으로 끌어올렸어요.

And Rapunzel ⬚ed Mother Gothel up into the tower.

5 라푼젤의 머리카락은 마력이 있었어요.

Rapunzel's hair was ⬚.

6 그것은 어머니 고델을 젊고 아름답게 유지해 주었어요.

It ⬚ Mother Gothel young and beautiful.

7 라푼젤은 어머니 고델이 라푼젤의 진짜 부모님인 왕과 왕비에게서 자신을 훔쳐왔다는 것을 알지 못했어요.

Rapunzel did not know that Mother Gothel had ⬚ her from her real parents, the King and the Queen.

8 어머니 고델은 그 마법 머리카락을 그녀 혼자서만 독차지하고 싶어 했어요.

Mother Gothel wanted the magical hair all for ⬚.

9 어머니 고델은 라푼젤을 탑에서 절대 내보내지 않았어요.

Mother Gothel never let Rapunzel ⬚ the tower.

10 그녀는 라푼젤에게 나쁜 사람들이 라푼젤의 마법 머리카락을 빼앗으려 한다고 말했어요.

She told Rapunzel that bad people wanted to ⬚ her magical hair.

Word Box

leave 통 떠나다	**as ~ as ...** ...만큼 ~한	**let** 통 ~하게 하다	**herself** 때 그녀 자신	**pull** 통 ~을 잡아당기다
stolen steal(훔치다)의 과거분사	**kept** keep(유지하다)의 과거형	**magical** 형 마력이 있는	**tower** 명 탑	**take** 통 가져가다

11 라푼젤에게는 친구가 하나 있었어요. 파스칼이라는 이름을 가진 카멜레온이었죠.

Rapunzel had one friend——a [   ] named Pascal.

12 일 년에 한 번 생일이 되면, 라푼젤은 하늘로 떠올라가는 반짝이는 불빛들을 보았어요.

Once a year, on her birthday, Rapunzel saw sparkling lights [   ]ing into the sky.

13 그녀는 탑을 떠나 그 불빛들을 더 가까이에서 볼 수 있으면 좋겠다고 생각했어요.

She wished she could leave the tower and see the lights [   ] [   ].

14 그 불빛들은 그녀에게 무엇인가를 의미하는 것 같았어요.

They seemed [   ] for her.

15 라푼젤의 열 여덟 번째 생일 직전에, 플린이라는 도둑이 숲을 가로질러 달리고 있었어요.

One day, just before Rapunzel's eighteenth birthday, a [   ] named Flynn was running through the forest.

16 그는 잃어버린 공주님의 왕관을 훔쳤어요.

He had stolen the [   ] princess's crown.

17 왕실 근위대의 과감한 말인 막시무스로부터 벗어나려 애쓰다가, 플린은 라푼젤의 숨겨진 탑을 발견했어요.

While trying to get away from Maximus, a determined horse from the royal guard, Flynn found Rapunzel's [   ] tower.

18 플린은 숨기 위해 그 탑을 타고 올라갔어요.

Flynn [   ]ed up the tower to hide.

19 라푼젤은 어머니 고델 외의 다른 사람은 한 번도 본 적이 없었어요.

Rapunzel had never seen another person [   ] Mother Gothel.

20 라푼젤은 플린이 자신의 머리카락을 원한다고 생각했어요. 하지만 플린은 머리카락을 원하지 않았어요.

Rapunzel [   ] Flynn wanted her hair. But he didn't.

Word Box

hidden	float	up close	chameleon	climb
형 숨겨진	통 (공중에서) 떠가다	바로 가까이에서	명 카멜레온	통 올라가다
lost	besides	thief	meant	thought
형 잃어버린	전 ~이외의	명 도둑	mean(의미하다)의 과거분사	think(생각하다)의 과거형

42

㉑ 라푼젤은 플린에게 불빛을 그린 그림을 보여주고, 그 불빛을 볼 수 있는 곳으로 데려가 달라고 부탁했어요.

Rapunzel [   ]ed Flynn a painting she had made of the lights and asked him to take her to see them.

㉒ 플린은 그러겠다고 했어요. 가는 길에, 플린과 라푼젤은 어떤 선술집에 들렀어요.

Flynn [   ]d. On the way, Flynn and Rapunzel stopped in a pub.

㉓ 그곳은 무섭게 생긴 남자들로 꽉 차 있었어요.

It was [   ]ed with scary-looking men.

㉔ 하지만 그들도 라푼젤의 머리카락을 훔치고 싶어 하지 않았어요. 그들은 친절했어요.

But they didn't want to steal Rapunzel's hair, either. They were [   ].

㉕ 막시무스와 왕실 근위대 병사들이 플린을 찾아냈어요.

Maximus and some royal guards [   ] Flynn.

㉖ 무섭게 생긴 남자들 중 한 명이 플린과 라푼젤이 달아나도록 도와주었어요.

One of the scary-looking men helped Flynn and Rapunzel [   ].

㉗ 그들은 달려가다가 물로 가득 찬 동굴 속에 갇혀버리고 말았어요.

They ran until they got trapped in a water-filled [   ].

㉘ 라푼젤의 환하게 빛나는 마법 머리카락은 동굴에서 나가는 길을 찾는 데 도움이 되었어요!

Rapunzel's magical [   ]ing hair helped them find a way out!

㉙ 하지만 막시무스가 플린을 또 찾아냈어요.

But Maximus found Flynn [   ].

㉚ 그 말은 플린을 감옥에 데려가려고 했어요. 라푼젤은 막시무스에게 오늘은 자신의 생일이라고 말했어요.

The horse wanted to take Flynn to [   ]. Rapunzel told Maximus it was her birthday.

Word Box

show 통 보여주다	found find(찾아내다)의 과거형	fill 통 가득 채우다	again 부 다시	cave 명 동굴
glow 통 빛나다	agree 통 동의하다	escape 통 달아나다	friendly 형 친절한	jail 명 감옥

31 라푼젤은 막시무스에게 부탁했어요. 플린이 자신을 반짝이는 불빛을 볼 수 있는 곳에 데려가게 해 달라고요.

She asked him to let Flynn take her to see the sparkling [   ]s.

32 막시무스는 그러겠다고 했어요. 라푼젤의 소원이 이루어질 참이었어요!

Maximus agreed. Rapunzel's [   ] was about to come true!

33 플린과 라푼젤은 아주 멋진 하루를 보냈어요.

Flynn and Rapunzel had a [   ] day.

34 한 어린 소년이 라푼젤에게 작은 왕국 국기를 주었어요.

A little boy gave Rapunzel a small kingdom [   ].

35 왕국에서는 잃어버린 공주의 생일을 기념하고 있었어요.

The kingdom was [   ] the birthday of the lost princess.

36 잃어버린 공주의 생일과 라푼젤의 생일은 같은 날이었어요!

The lost princess had the [   ] birthday as Rapunzel!

37 라푼젤은 왕과 왕비가 아기 공주님을 안고 있는 그림을 보았어요.

Rapunzel saw a picture of the King and the Queen [   ]ing their baby princess.

38 왕비와 공주님은 라푼젤과 똑같은 초록색 눈을 가지고 있었어요!

The Queen and the Princess had green eyes——just [   ] Rapunzel!

39 갑작스럽게 라푼젤은 자신도 모르게 휩쓸려 춤을 추게 되었어요!

[   ], Rapunzel was swept up in a dance!

40 그녀는 인생에서 가장 재미있는 시간을 보냈어요! 지금까지는 말이에요.

It was the most [   ] she had ever had... so far.

Word Box

flag	hold	wonderful	celebrating	wish
명 국기	동 잡고 있다	형 아주 멋진	celebrate(기념하다)의 진행형	명 소원
same	fun	just like	suddenly	light
형 똑같은	형 재미있는	마치 ~처럼	부 갑자기	명 불빛

41 그날 밤, 왕국 사람들은 등불을 밝혔어요.

That night, the people of the kingdom [   ] lanterns.

42 마침내 라푼젤의 소원이 이루어졌어요.

[   ] [   ] , Rapunzel's wish came true.

43 매우 기뻐하며 그녀는 하늘을 가득 메운 반짝이는 불빛들을 보았어요.

[   ] , she saw the sparkling lights fill the sky.

44 그녀는 탑 밖의 세상이 너무나 좋았어요.

She loved the world [   ] the tower.

45 그녀는 플린을 사랑했어요. 그리고 플린도 그녀를 사랑했어요.

She loved Flynn. And he loved her, [   ] .

46 해안가에서 플린은 라푼젤의 곁을 떠나 돌아오지 않았어요.

On [   ] , Flynn left Rapunzel and did not return.

47 라푼젤은 마음이 아팠어요.

Rapunzel was [   ] .

48 그녀는 플린이 사악한 어머니 고델의 계략에 속아 넘어갔다는 사실을 알지 못했어요.

She did not know that Flynn had been [   ] ed by evil Mother Gothel.

49 그는 체포되어 감옥에 갇혔던 거예요!

He had been [   ] d and put in jail!

50 어머니 고델은 라푼젤을 찾아내서 탑으로 다시 데려갔어요.

Mother Gothel [   ] Rapunzel and took her back to the tower.

Word Box

found find(찾아내다)의 과거형	at last 뷔 마침내	outside 혱 외부의	overjoyed 혱 매우 기뻐하는	heartbroken 혱 가슴 아픈
shore 몡 해안	too 뷔 ~도 또한	trick 통 속이다	capture 통 체포하다	lit light(불을 붙이다)의 과거형

51 방으로 돌아온 라푼젤은 자신이 평생동안 왕국의 상징인 황금빛 태양을 벽에 그려왔다는 것을 깨달았어요!

Back in her room, Rapunzel realized that she had been painting the kingdom's _____, the golden sun, on her wall her entire life!

52 라푼젤은 잃어버린 공주와 왕비의 그림을 기억해 냈어요.

Rapunzel _____ed the picture of the lost princess and the Queen.

53 라푼젤은 이제 그들이 왜 비슷하게 닮아 보였는지 알게 되었어요.

Now Rapunzel knew why they all looked _____.

54 어머니 고델만이 라푼젤의 마법 머리카락을 훔치고 싶어하는 유일한 사람이었어요.

Mother Gothel was the _____ one who wanted to steal Rapunzel's magical hair.

55 그녀는 라푼젤에게 거짓말만 했던 거예요. "어머니, 제가 바로 잃어버린 공주군요." 라푼젤은 말했어요.

She had _____d to Rapunzel about everything. "Mother, I am the lost princess," Rapunzel said.

56 한편, 플린은 감옥을 탈출해서 라푼젤을 구하기 위해 탑에 도착했어요.

Meanwhile, Flynn had escaped and arrived at the tower to _____ Rapunzel.

57 "라푼젤! 라푼젤! 머리카락을 내려 줘요!" 그가 외쳤어요. 그러나 어머니 고델은 라푼젤을 놓아주려 하지 않았어요.

"Rapunzel! Rapunzel! Let down your hair!" he called. But Mother Gothel would not _____ Rapunzel go.

58 어머니 고델은 플린이 다시는 라푼젤을 자신에게서 빼앗아가지 못하도록 그에게 큰 상처를 입혔어요.

Mother Gothel _____ Flynn so badly that he could never, ever take Rapunzel from her.

59 그러나 플린에게는 라푼젤을 구해낼 방법이 하나 있었어요.

Flynn still thought of a way to _____ Rapunzel.

Word Box

save 동 구하다	remember 동 기억하다	lie 동 거짓말하다	only 형 유일한	let 동 ~하게 해주다
emblem 명 상징	alike 형 비슷한	hurt hurt(다치게 하다)의 과거형	rescue 동 구출하다	

46

60 그는 그녀의 머리카락을 잘랐어요. 라푼젤의 마법 머리카락이 없어지자, 어머니 고델은 힘없이 죽어갔어요.

He cut her hair. Without Rapunzel's magical hair, Mother Gothel [   ]ed away.

61 라푼젤은 마침내 사악한 여자로부터 자유로워졌어요.

Rapunzel was finally [   ] of the evil woman.

62 하지만 긴 머리카락이 없으니 플린을 구할 마력도 더는 없었어요.

But [   ] her long hair, Rapunzel had no more magic to save Flynn.

63 그는 결국 눈을 감았어요.

He [   ]d his eyes for the last time.

64 라푼젤은 울었어요. 황금 눈물 한 방울이 플린의 뺨에 떨어졌어요.

Rapunzel cried. A [   ] golden tear fell on Flynn's cheek.

65 눈물에는 라푼젤 안에 남아 있던 마지막 한 방울의 마력이 담겨 있었어요.

It [   ]ed the last bit of magic left inside Rapunzel.

66 플린은 눈을 떴어요! 그는 무사했어요!

Flynn's eyes [   ]ed! He was all right!

67 라푼젤은 그녀의 진짜 부모님인 왕과 왕비에게 갔어요.

Rapunzel went to her [   ] parents, the King and the Queen.

68 18년을 기다린 끝에, 왕과 왕비는 초록색 눈의 소녀를 한 번 보고는 그녀가 자신들의 딸임을 알아챘어요.

After eighteen years of waiting, they took one look at the green-eyed girl and knew she was their [   ].

69 마침내 라푼젤은 집에 돌아왔어요!

Rapunzel had come [   ] at last!

Word Box

wither 통 시들다, 말라 죽다	**single** 형 단 하나의	**without** 전 ~없이	**close** 통 닫다, (눈을) 감다	**real** 형 진짜의, 실제의
open 통 열다, (눈을) 뜨다	**contain** 통 ~을 포함하다	**free** 형 자유로운	**daughter** 명 딸	**home** 부 집으로

70 라푼젤은 그녀의 새로운 삶이 정말 좋았어요. 그녀는 탑 밖의 세상을 사랑했어요.

Rapunzel loved her [   ] life. She loved the world outside the tower.

71 그녀는 새로운 친구들을 사랑했어요. 마침내 그녀는 자신이 있어야 할 곳이 어디인지 알게 되었어요.

She loved her new friends. At last, she knew where she [   ]ed.

72 그리고 그 후 그들은 모두 행복하게 살았답니다.

And they all lived [   ] ever after.

48

TOY STORY 4

빈칸에 알맞은 단어를 채워 문장을 완성하세요.

1 안녕, 파트너!

_____, partner!

2 이 구역의 보안관인 우디와 인사하세요.

Meet Woody, the _____ round these parts.

3 우디는 자신의 주인 아이인 앤디를 사랑했고, 앤디 방에 있는 장난감들의 대표였어요.

Woody loved his kid, Andy, and was the _____ of the toys in Andy's room.

4 하지만 때때로 그는 도움이 필요할 때가 있었어요.

But sometimes he _____ed help.

5 고맙게도 그의 가장 친한 친구인 보핍은 늘 도움을 주었죠.

Thankfully, his best friend, Bo Peep, was always there to lend a _____.

6 그러던 어느 날, 모든 게 바뀌어 버렸어요.

Then one day, everything _____d.

7 보핍은 새 주인을 만나게 되었고 우디는 뒤에 남겨졌어요.

Bo Peep was getting a new kid——and Woody was staying _____.

8 몇 년 후, 우디에게도 새로운 주인 아이가 생겼어요. 그 여자 아이의 이름은 보니였어요.

Years _____, Woody got a new kid, too. Her name was Bonnie.

9 유치원 예비 소집일에 그 여자 아이는 조금 긴장했어요.

At kindergarten _____, she was a little nervous.

10 다행히도 그녀 주변에는 보안관 하나가 있었죠!

Luckily, she had a sheriff _____!

Word Box

behind	sheriff	hand	orientation	Howdy
〉 뒤에	〉 보안관	〉 도움	〉 예비 소집	안녕
change	leader	later	around	need
〉 변하다	〉 대표, 지도자	〉 후에, 나중에	〉 주변에 있는	〉 필요로 하다

11. 한 남자 아이가 보니의 미술도구를 가져가버리자 우디가 도구를 재빨리 마련해 줬어요. 새로운 도구들과 함께요.

When a boy took her art supplies, Woody [   ]d them up, along with some new ones.

12. 보니는 상상력을 발휘해서 도구들을 모아 새로운 친구를 만들었어요.

Bonnie used her imagination to put them [   ] to make a new friend.

13. 놀랍게도, 포키가 살아났어요. 다른 장난감들처럼요!

To Woody's surprise, Forky came to [   ]——just like the other toys!

14. 포키도 역시 놀랐어요.

Forky was [   ], too.

15. 그는 자기 자신을 장난감이라고 생각하지 않았어요. 그는 포크 겸용 숟가락이었거든요!

He didn't think he was a toy at all——he was a [   ]!

16. 그래서 보니의 가족이 레저용 자동차를 타고 장거리 자동차 여행을 떠났을 때, 포키는 도망치려 했어요!

So when Bonnie's family went on a [   ] [   ] in their RV... Forky made a break for it!

17. 보안관 우디는 절대로 누군가를 두고 가는 법이 없었어요.

Sheriff Woody would never [   ] anyone behind.

18. 그는 포키를 쫓아 창 밖으로 뛰어 나갔어요. 우디는 보니를 따라잡기 위해 포키를 데리고 옆 도시로 갔어요.

He jumped out the window after Forky. Woody took Forky to the next town to [   ] up with Bonnie.

19. 그러다 골동품 상점 창가에 있는 무언가가 우디의 눈길을 끌었어요. 보의 램프였어요!

Then something in the window of an [   ] store caught his eye... Bo's lamp!

20. 우디와 포키는 상점 안으로 들어갔어요. 보를 찾는 것 대신, 그들은 개비 개비라는 이름의 인형을 보았어요.

Woody and Forky went into the store. [   ] of finding Bo, they saw a doll named Gabby Gabby.

Word Box

rustle up ~을 급히 찾아주다	**put together** (이것저것을 모아) 만들다	**catch** 통 잡다	**antiques** 명 골동품	**spork** 명 포크 겸용 숟가락
surprised 형 놀란	**road trip** 명 장거리 자동차 여행	**life** 명 삶, 생명	**leave** 통 ~을 떠나다	**instead** 부 대신에

21 그녀는 처음엔 친절해 보였어요. 하지만 다음에 그녀는 우디의 소리 장치를 원한다고 말했어요.

She seemed [_____] at first——but then she said she wanted Woody's voice box.

22 그녀는 자신의 팀에게 우디와 포키를 붙잡으라고 했어요!

She told her team to [_____] Woody and Forky!

23 우디는 근처의 놀이터로 도망쳤고 그곳에서 낯익은 얼굴을 보았어요. 보핍이었죠!

Woody escaped to a nearby playground, where he saw a [_____] face——Bo Peep!

24 그녀와 아주 작은 친구 기글 맥딤플즈는 한 무리의 장난감들과 여행 중이었어요. 같이 놀 주인 아이를 찾기 위해서요.

She and her tiny friend, Giggle McDimples, were [_____]ing with a group of toys to find kids to play with.

25 보는 우디가 포키를 구하는 것을 돕겠다고 말했어요!

Bo said she would help Woody [_____] Forky!

26 한편 버즈 라이트이어는 우디와 포키를 찾고 있었어요. 그 용감한 우주 전사는 그들의 흔적을 따라서 축제장에 왔지만, 경품벽에 붙어버리고 말았어요.

Meanwhile, Buzz Lightyear was searching for Woody and Forky. The brave space ranger followed their [_____] to a carnival, but he got stuck to a prize wall.

27 그는 더키와 버니라는 장난감들을 만났어요.

He [_____] a couple of toys, Ducky and Bunny.

28 버즈는 어쩌다 보니 그 둘을 자유롭게 풀어 주었어요!

Buzz accidentally set both of them [_____]!

29 버즈는 우디와 보를 발견했고, 그들 모두는 골동품 상점 안으로 살금살금 들어갔어요.

Buzz found Woody and Bo, and the whole group [_____]ed into the antiques store.

Word Box

trail	**friendly**	**familiar**	**sneak**	**rescue**
몡 흔적	혱 친절한	혱 익숙한	통 살금살금 가다	통 구출하다
free	**met**	**capture**	**travel**	
통 풀어 주다	meet(만나다)의 과거형	통 붙잡다	통 여행하다	

30 포키는 높은 수납장 안에 갇혀 있었어요.

Forky was trapped in a tall [　　　　].

31 상점의 고양이인 드래곤이 복도를 돌아다녔어요. 한 입에 꿀꺽할 길 잃은 장난감들을 찾아서요.

The store's cat, Dragon, [　　　　]ed the aisles, looking for stray toys to gobble up.

32 친구들은 계획을 생각해내야 했어요.

The friends had to [　　　　] out a plan.

33 보는 캐나다에서 제일가는 스턴트맨인 듀크 카붐을 찾아냈어요.

Bo found Duke Caboom, Canada's greatest [　　　　].

34 그는 보의 양들뿐만 아니라 포키를 구하는 것을 도와줄 거예요. 그들도 잡혀 있었거든요.

He would help rescue Forky, as well as Bo's [　　　　]. They had been captured, too.

35 듀크는 복도를 가로질러 수납장을 향해 뛰어올랐어요.

Duke [　　　　]ed across the aisle to the cabinet.

36 하지만 그는 성공하지 못했어요.

But he didn't [　　　　] it.

37 드래곤이 그와 장난감들을 발견한 거예요!

Dragon [　　　　]ted him and the toys!

38 드래곤이 듀크를 쫓기 시작한 바로 그때, 보가 그녀의 양들을 발견했어요.

Bo found her sheep just as Dragon began to [　　　　] Duke.

39 인형들은 꽉 붙잡았어요!

The toys held on [　　　　]!

Word Box

cabinet 명 수납장	**stuntman** 명 스턴트맨, 대역	**figure out** 생각해 내다	**roam** 통 돌아다니다	**chase** 통 뒤쫓다
leap 통 뛰어오르다	**sheep** 명 양, 양들	**spot** 통 발견하다	**make it** 성공하다	**tight** 부 단단히, 꽉

52

40 그들은 상점 밖으로 나오는 데 성공했지만, 포키는 아직 그 안에 있었어요.

They made it out of the store——but Forky was still [   ].

41 친구들 대부분은 너무 피곤하고 무서워서 새로운 계획을 시도할 수가 없었어요.

Most of the group was too tired and scared to [   ] a new plan.

42 그들은 떠나기로 결정했어요. 하지만 우디는 포키를 데려와야 했어요.

They [   ]d to leave. But Woody needed to get Forky.

43 그는 개비 개비와 거래를 했어요.

He made a [   ] with Gabby Gabby.

44 포키를 받는 대신, 그는 그녀에게 그의 소리 장치를 주었어요.

In [   ] for Forky, he gave her his voice box.

45 우디는 개비 개비가 주인 아이를 가질 수 있도록 그녀를 보니에게 데려다 주기로 했어요. 장난감들은 우디와 개비 개비를 도우러 다시 돌아왔어요.

And he would take her to Bonnie so she could have a kid, too. The toys [   ]ed to help Woody and Gabby Gabby.

46 하지만 보니에게 이르는 방법은 단 하나뿐이었어요.

But there was only one way to [   ] Bonnie.

47 그들은 축제장으로 가서 대관람차의 꼭대기에 올랐어요.

They went to the carnival and rode to the [   ] of the Ferris wheel.

48 그런 다음 듀크의 자전거에 긴 끈을 둘러 묶었어요.

Then they tied a long [   ] around Duke's bike.

49 듀크는 숨을 깊이 들이마시고 엔진의 속도를 올렸어요. 그리고 사람들 위로 날아올랐어요!

Duke took a deep breath, revved his engine and [   ]ed over the crowd!

Word Box

inside	exchange	decide	top	try
분 안에	명 교환	동 결정하다	명 꼭대기	동 시도하다
string	**reach**	**deal**	**return**	**soar**
명 끈	동 ~에 이르다	명 거래	동 돌아오다	동 날아오르다

50 듀크 덕분에, 장난감들은 줄에 매달려 축제장을 쌩 하고 지나갈 수 있었어요.

_____ to Duke, the toys zipped across the carnival on the string.

51 개비 개비는 길을 잃어 친구를 필요로 하는 한 소녀를 발견했어요.

Then Gabby Gabby _____d a girl who was lost and needed a friend.

52 개비 개비는 그 소녀에게 완벽했어요!

Gabby Gabby was _____ for her!

53 소녀는 개비 개비를 꼭 껴안았고, 곧바로 자신의 부모님을 찾았어요. 개비 개비에게도 주인 아이가 생겼어요!

The girl hugged the doll close just before she found her _____. Gabby Gabby got a kid!

54 장난감들은 보니를 찾았어요. 보니는 포키를 다시 만나 신이 났어요!

The toys found Bonnie. She was _____ to see Forky again!

55 우디는 그 둘이 행복해하는 모습을 보고 기분이 좋았어요. 또 그의 친구들과 다시 만나게 되어 기뻤어요.

Woody loved seeing the two of them so happy. And he was glad to be _____d with his friends.

56 우디는 길을 잃고 외로운 장난감들이 어디에나 있다는 사실을 깨달았고, 그들을 돕고 싶어졌어요.

Woody _____d that lost and lonely toys were everywhere, and he wanted to help them.

57 그는 보와 그들의 친구들과 함께라면 어떤 일이든 해낼 수 있을 거라는 사실을 알게 되었어요!

He knew with Bo and their friends, he could _____ anything!

Word Box

thanks to ~의 덕분에	**notice** 통 발견하다, 알아채다	**thrilled** 형 신이 난	**perfect** 형 완벽한
accomplish 통 해내다, 성취하다	**realize** 통 깨닫다	**parents** 명 부모	**reunite** 통 다시 만나다

Disney · PIXAR
Story Collection 1

Practice Book

Part 1 단어 연습 (Word Practice)

스토리북에 등장한 핵심 어휘를 익힙니다. 어려운 단어들을 순서대로 정리해 보고,
이 외에도 잘 모르는 단어는 사전에서 찾아 뜻과 철자를 기록합니다.

Part 2 전체 문장 연습 (Sentence Practice)

읽은 내용을 다시 떠올리며 우리말에 맞도록 문장을 완성합니다.
빈칸에 들어갈 알맞은 단어를 찾는 과정에서 문장 구조와 표현을 익힐 수 있습니다.